RETIRE
WITHOUT WORRY

Simple, Straightforward Answers to
Serious Financial Questions

Robert J. Reby
Certified Financial Planner

R. J. REBY FOUNDATION, INC.
DANBURY, CONNECTICUT

ISBN 0-9740163-0-6

First Edition
10 9 8 7 6 5 4 3 2 1

The publisher offers quantity discounts on this book. For information, contact:
R. J. Reby Foundation, Inc.
83 Wooster Heights Road
Danbury, CT 06810
203-744-2121
www.rjrebyfoundation.org

Publishing Consultant: Neuhaus Publishing
Editor: Tom Nawrocki
Cover Design: Codesign
Interior Design and Composition: Ed Kotzen

CONTENTS

Acknowledgments

I want to take a moment and thank some of the people who have helped me complete this book. Ed Frede, the respected journalist and past editor of the *Danbury News Times* (Danbury, Connecticut) called me in 1994 and asked me to be a contributing columnist to our city's newspaper. That was a tremendous opportunity. Writing a weekly column gave me even more insight into people's concerns and issues, and it allowed me to grow and explore new ideas. In fact, those columns form the core of this book. Thank you, Ed!

A special thanks to Trudy Neuhaus, Tom Nawrocki, Gaye Carleton, Donna Muro, Loreen Lewis, Dawn Rancourt, Kristina TenEyck, Jennifer Masterson, and Jacqueline Endlich. As a team, they have helped me enormously. Whether they were providing advice, acting as another set of eyes, or facilitating the process, they helped me to stay focused and persevere.

Finally, my wife, Mary, let me work on this book on our vacations and weekends, which often was the only time I had to devote to it. Thank you, Mary, for your support and patience.

INTRODUCTION

Considering the wealth of retirement information that's available today, I'm always somewhat surprised that so many people still have so many questions. But, in fact, they do. Every day, clients ask me questions, as do colleagues, friends, family members—even people I've just met.

Why is this?

One reason is the ever-increasing interest in retirement planning. More and more people of every age and income bracket are thinking about that point down the road when they can or must stop working. This is a very positive trend, because it's necessary: It's up to each of us to provide for our own retirement.

Another reason is because retirement issues are increasingly complex. It wasn't so long ago that you could consider yourself set if you were making contributions to a 401(k) or equivalent plan and an IRA. Now, it's not so simple. Are your contributions invested wisely? Should you leave your retirement plans invested with ex-employers or roll them over to your new employer? How will taxes affect the return on your investments or the inheritance your beneficiaries receive? These are just a few of the many issues each of us must address today.

Oddly enough, once you retire it doesn't get any simpler. When's the best time to begin making withdrawals from your IRA? What's the best way to help a grandchild pay for schooling? Is a will the best way to bequeath your estate to your beneficiaries? It can seem like the more you learn the more questions you have.

Still another reason is that things change—or appear to change. Just when you think you know what to do, the market declines, the market rises, a new theory circulates, another alternative is promoted, or a new tax law is introduced. One day you're sure you've made the right decisions, and the next you're back to researching your options.

More surprising than the sheer number of questions, however, is how often they are the same and asked year after year. That's what prompted me to write this book. During my eighteen years as a certified financial planner, I've written a newspaper column, hosted a radio program, given numerous seminars, and been interviewed by local and national magazine, radio, and television journalists. No matter the forum, people often raise the same issues and concerns again and again. This book encapsulates this experience. It is a compilation of more than 250 simple, straightforward answers to serious financial questions that I've been asked most frequently.

If your goal is to retire without worry, this book can help. I've organized the book into nine popular topic areas using a question and answer format. If you're looking for a particular answer, the Q&A format lets you browse the text and quickly find the information you need. In addition, you can familiarize yourself with topics and issues by reading through the questions others have asked.

When you think about retiring, the first thing that probably comes to mind is investing. To some extent you're right: To maintain your lifestyle during retirement, the income you earn on your savings needs to outpace rising prices and taxes. Investing has long been the best way to stay ahead of inflation. The first three sections of this book cover the most common investment vehicles for individuals: stocks, bonds, and mutual funds.

Equally important, however, is *how* you invest. The fourth section covers investing concepts and strategies, such as asset allocation and diversification.

If your retirement plan boils down to accumulating as much money as possible between now and then, you'll want to read Section 5, "Retirement Planning." Investors often take chances that jeopardize their retirement savings simply because they don't know how much money they'll need. Don't take unnecessary risks; make sure you have a retirement plan.

You might think that after you retire, your plan kicks in and you won't have to pay as close attention to your financial matters as you do now. In reality, retirement often raises a whole new set of questions you hadn't thought about before. You can read about some of these in Section 6, "Retirement."

After working hard to save and accumulate assets, you want to make sure they are passed along to your beneficiaries according to your wishes, and that, now or later, the IRS doesn't get more of your hard-earned dollars than it should. Sections 7 and 8 provide answers to questions on estate planning and taxes, respectively.

All of the previous topics come under the giant heading of financial planning. It's a big job, but someone has to do it. Whether you decide to undertake this exercise yourself or enlist the help of a financial advisor, read Section 9, "Financial Planning." It has helpful tips on creating a plan as well as finding, hiring, and working with a certified financial planner.

Everyone has questions about retiring and, in a way, it's comforting to know that for many of us they are the same or similar. But that won't alleviate your specific concerns. The only way you can put your mind at ease—and begin looking forward to retirement—is to educate yourself about the alternatives, have a plan, follow it, and stick to it. I encourage you to read this book and others, talk to a certified financial planner, realistically assess your situation, and understand your options. Once you do, you'll be on the road to retiring without worry.

SECTION 1

~

STOCKS

7 RULES FOR STOCK INVESTORS

➤ Invest in equities for the rest of your life

➤ Invest using dollar-cost averaging

➤ Don't try to time the market

➤ Diversify

➤ Take advantage of professional management

➤ Don't make decisions based on the emotions of fear or greed

➤ Consider consulting with a financial advisor

A large and important part of most investors' portfolio is their stock holdings. This is as it should be, because for most people the stock market represents a good opportunity to provide the kind of returns that can make them financially secure. So it's not surprising that one of the most common questions people ask me concerns their fear of a market decline: What should I do when the market corrects itself?

I've long argued that investors shouldn't fear a market decline; indeed, in a lot of ways, it's a good thing for the long-term investor. I explain that outlook in this section, as well as how to find and evaluate stocks, what your investments in the market really mean, and how the overall U.S. economy relates to the market's performance. We also take a look at some key sectors of the market, such as tech stocks, utilities, and brand-name multinationals. I begin by giving you my six rules for investing in stocks—and by the time you finish reading this section, you'll see why a long-term stock investor is the best kind to be.

In this section, you'll see the words "stocks" and "equities" both used, but don't be confused: These are two terms for the same thing, an ownership stake in a publicly held company. We also use the term "securities," which is an investment category that includes stocks, bonds, and a few other things as well.

I MISSED OUT ON THE GREAT RETURNS IN THE STOCK MARKET DURING THE LATTER PART OF THE '90S, BUT I AM READY TO INVEST NOW. HOW SHOULD I BEGIN?

Here are my six time-tested rules for stock investors:

1. **Invest for the long term.** The best way to reduce the risks of stocks and enhance potential returns is to invest long term, rather than buying a stock because you think it's about to increase in value and planning to sell it when it does—a short-term strategy. Since 1926, all the twenty-year rolling time periods—1926 to 1945, 1927 to 1946, and so on—have been positive for the S&P 500 index, and 89 percent of the five-year periods were positive.
2. **Invest using dollar-cost averaging.** Dollar-cost averaging means investing a fixed amount on a regular schedule, such as monthly. It is a simple, practical, and recommended way to invest. If you invest using dollar-cost averaging, you are

employing a strategic and financially sound investment method, rather than being enticed to invest by the success of the market—when prices are high—and being frightened into selling—or not buying—when prices are low. Dollar-cost averaging doesn't assure a profit or protect against a loss in a declining market, and you need to consider your ability to invest consistently in a downturn, but it does help protect against emotions influencing investment decisions.

3. **Don't try to time the market.** Some investors try to buy into the market, or buy particular stocks, when prices are at their lowest, and sell when the market reaches its peak, a practice known as timing the market. The market and stock prices are hard to predict, however. Just when you think they can't drop any lower, they do, and when you think they're at their peak, they climb higher. Stay your course, and you won't miss regular opportunities to add to your holdings when prices are low.

4. **Diversify.** Buy many different types of securities across a variety of investment categories and industries and, if you're interested, a variety of global markets as well. This can help control the overall volatility of your investments.

5. **Take advantage of the professional management that investing in a stock mutual fund affords.** If a professional increases your bottom line even by a mere 1 percent a year, that has the potential to increase your portfolio's value by thousands of dollars over time. While it's important to evaluate a stock fund's objectives (whether it seeks growth, income, or some combination of the two) and management style (whether it looks for undervalued companies—value stocks—or growing ones—growth stocks), it is also important to look for an investment company with a record of good performance over the long term. At the same time, though, you need to remember that past performance is no guarantee of future results. Investment firms have literature on their funds' performance as well as their management styles, and they're happy to send it to you with a call to their 800 number or a visit to their Web site.

6. **Consider consulting with a financial advisor.** A financial advisor who is working for you and aware of your goals and concerns, can help you stay the course and continue investing through the market's normal ups and downs. I have

found that much of the value of a good and trusted financial
advisor comes from instilling confidence in the plan when
need be, helping clients find opportunities in a volatile marketplace, and educating clients to prevent them from shoot-
ing themselves in the foot.

*I HAVE READ THAT EQUITIES ARE AN IMPORTANT PART OF A LONG-TERM
INVESTMENT PLAN, BUT I AM CONCERNED ABOUT RISKING MY MONEY
AND LOSING IT. WHAT MAKES THEM SO VITAL?*

Historically, equity investments have proven to generate higher
long-term returns than most other alternatives. Just to break
even with a hypothetical 5 percent rate of inflation and a combined tax bracket of 40 percent, you need to achieve a rate of
return of 8.3 percent annually. Although past performance is no
guarantee of future results, equities are the only asset class that
has provided high enough returns to match that need.

Here is a story that illustrates my point. In 1969, a $100,000
Certificate of Deposit (CD) would have generated enough interest
in one year at an average rate of 7.9 percent to buy a brand new,
fully-loaded, hardtop Cadillac Sedan DeVille at a cost of $5,936.
In 1997, that same $100,000 CD, although insured and guaran-
teed, wouldn't generate enough income to buy one-eighth of that
same Cadillac. The average CD rate then was 4.95 percent, in
part because inflation was so much lower in 1997, and the cost of
the 1997 DeVille was approximately $43,000, due in part to infla-
tion in the intervening years.

This example of inflation risk is a powerful reason for you to
consider including stocks as part of your overall investment
strategy. Although stock prices will fluctuate, the cost of items
you need will also rise over time. On a historical basis, stocks
have provided a high enough return to preserve your consumer
purchasing power. Only by staying well ahead of rising costs will
you be able to have the lifestyle you want during retirement.

IF STOCKS ARE MY ONLY REAL HEDGE AGAINST INFLATION, WHY SHOULD I INVEST IN ANYTHING ELSE?

While inflation may be the biggest threat to your investments, it's not the only one. In a bear market, stocks often decline in value and bonds often increase in value. For long-term investors, it's highly unlikely that you would lose money in the stock market over a ten- or twenty-year period, but if you're investing for the near term—say you're three years from retirement—you can always use some extra protection. That's why a common rule of thumb is that the percentage of your portfolio in stocks should be 100 minus your age, so that the nearer you get to retirement, the less you are subject to the volatility of the market.

WHEN INFLATION RISES, STOCK PRICES FALL. WHY THEN ARE STOCKS OR STOCK MUTUAL FUNDS USUALLY RECOMMENDED AS A GOOD WAY TO PROTECT OUR PURCHASING POWER OVER TIME?

The best way to answer your question is to first distinguish between short-term market fluctuations and long-term investment results. In the short term, the threat of inflation makes the stock market nervous. Because anyone who buys stock in a company is really paying for that company's anticipated future earnings, and inflation can reduce the expected value of those earnings, the threat of inflation can erode a stock's present value. However, the threat of inflation usually doesn't make stock prices fall for an extended period.

U.S. companies also have a long history of increasing dividends over time. Dividends from the stock market more than quadrupled during the twenty years ending in 1996. So, if you do your homework and choose companies that are positioned for future market share and profit increases, you could reasonably expect more dividend growth over time, and growing dividends can allow you more income to keep pace with the ravages of taxes and rising prices.

IS IT SENSIBLE TO MAKE A LUMP-SUM INVESTMENT IN THE MARKET?

The advantage of a lump-sum investment, which puts a large amount of money to work all at once, is that it can give you a return on your investment relatively quickly; the disadvantage is that you may purchase near the peak of a cycle and have to ride out a correction before seeing your investment appreciate.

You can avoid buying at the top by investing using dollar-cost averaging, one of my six rules for stock investors. This simply means investing a fixed amount at regular intervals. Naturally, a set amount will buy fewer shares of stock or a mutual fund when prices are relatively high, and more shares when prices are low. Therefore, you must stick to your investment schedule over a period of time in up and down markets to reap the full benefit. Dollar-cost averaging also reduces the temptation to let your emotional reactions dictate investment decisions. Of course, this approach does not assure you of a gain or protect you from a loss.

I HAVE A LOT OF MONEY IN A PARTICULAR FUND. THE PORTFOLIO MANAGER WHO MANAGES THIS FUND DOESN'T GET OUT OF STOCKS WHEN THE MARKET FALLS. WHY DON'T PROFESSIONALS KNOW BETTER?

Many people ask me this question. When evaluating a portfolio manager's actions, it's important to remember that many managers who are handling stock portfolios for thousands, or even millions of Americans, have successfully managed money for decades—long before I was even in Little League. So there is a method to their madness. Let me explain their thinking.

Portfolio managers who have a proven, time-tested, disciplined money management style do not normally convert shares to cash when the stock market declines significantly. To the contrary: What they do, in most cases, is buy more shares of the same businesses they already own. Here's why: They bought the companies they own because they analyzed them and decided that these stocks are either worth more than the market thinks (value stocks) or are capable of continued growth in the future (growth stocks). Hence, when the market declines, they buy more.

Put yourself in their shoes and let's say that you had found one hundred companies that were good investments at $50 per share. You purchase shares in these companies only to see the stock prices decline 20 percent to $40 per share, mostly because of an overall market downturn. You have confidence in these businesses, however, and are confident that these stocks will appreciate in the long run. Hence, shares that were a good buy at $50 look to be an even better buy at $40. Food for thought.

WHY DO MARKET DROPS SCARE PEOPLE IF THEY'RE SUCH GREAT OPPORTUNITIES FOR LONG-TERM INVESTORS?

Market drops often scare investors, because they are focusing on the short term and not the long term. Rather than looking for good buys when the market drops, investors often focus on the drop in value of their stocks and forget that over time, the market can come back and stocks may regain their value. The fear that grips investors is often encouraged by the media, which focuses on the short term and the crisis of the moment, rather than the long term.

WHAT IS A STOCK MARKET CORRECTION? IT SOUNDS LIKE A EUPHEMISM FOR CRASH.

In good times, investors consistently see balances on their portfolio statements that exceed those of the period before. Soon they come to expect this and forget that price declines result from what I consider normal corrections. Normal corrections are the digestion process of the investment markets, or the sometimes herky-jerky movement of stock prices as they try to find their true value.

From time to time, the markets turn down, sometimes dramatically. There is no official scale, but a normal correction is a drop of 5 percent or less, a moderate correction is a decline of 10 percent or less, and a severe correction may be a decline of 15 percent or more.

While it is uncomfortable to hear daily news reports of declines in major stock market averages, this should not be seen as a reason to panic and take action. That could very well be in conflict with your long-term, best interests as an investor. Table 1-1 shows how the market has reacted to several crises in recent history.

Table 1-1: Performance After a Crisis (Performance of the Dow Jones Industrial Average through Six Major Postwar Crises)

Crisis	One Year Later	Two Years Later
Korean War	+28.8%	+39.3%
Cuban Missile Crisis	+33.8%	+57.3%
Kennedy Assassination	+25.0%	+33.0%
1973-74 Stock Market Break	+42.2%	+66.5%
1979-80 Oil Crisis	+27.9%	+5.9%
1990 Persian Gulf War	+23.6%	+31.3%
Average Appreciation	+29.2%	+41.0%

Data obtained from Ibbotson Associates, Inc.
* The Dow Jones Industrial Average is an unmanaged stock index. Investors cannot directly invest in the DJIA. Past performance is not indicative of future results. Performance reflects appreciation only; does not include dividends.

WHAT SHOULD BE MY STRATEGY WHEN A CORRECTION HAPPENS?

During a correction, don't abandon your regular investing principles. If you are investing in mutual funds using a method such as dollar-cost averaging, for example, you should stay with it if possible. You need to consider your financial ability to continue investing through economic down times, of course, but remember that those fixed-dollar amounts buy more shares when prices are falling. If you are fairly confident about your financial situation and can afford to increase the amount you invest, you might consider taking advantage of the opportunities that a correction offers.

If you don't have time to research companies or funds for possible investment, consult a financial advisor. He or she may be able to help you find some undervalued stocks. Above all, though, remember that while a stock market downturn can be uncomfortable, it is not a time for hasty actions, particularly if you have developed a disciplined, long-term investment program designed to weather short-term market changes.

I HAVE HEARD YOU SAY THAT YOU WELCOME BEAR MARKETS. WHY WOULD YOU WANT TO SEE A SIGNIFICANT MARKET DECLINE?

I do welcome bear markets, and so should any long-term investor. I get some unusual looks whenever I make this comment, but before I explain my thinking let me define what a bear market is. A bear market is a stock market decline of 20 percent or more that lasts at least several months.

Now, bear markets always rattle some cages and create quite a stir. So why do I welcome them? There are several reasons. First, it is healthy—even essential—for the market to digest its gains, which is what it's doing in a bear market.

Second, a significant stock market decline usually restores realistic investor expectations of performance. In recent bull markets, investors have become accustomed to high returns and forgotten that 10 percent is an average return; instead, they have seen it as a floor. That is not realistic and often leads these investors to make foolish choices as they chase perennial 25 percent gains. The returns on equities are rewards for an investor's willingness and ability to withstand equity volatility over a period of many years. It is not reasonable to expect high returns—or even positive returns. This point was lost in the mid to late 1990s.

Third, a bear market often causes investors to rethink their goals. In bull markets, performance often becomes the goal. Investors forget their real objectives—such as to be financially secure and maintain their lifestyle in retirement—and focus on earning the maximum return. In bear markets, investors calculate the cost of their retirement, make adjustments for inflation, analyze how much money they have now and how much they plan to save before retirement, and then determine the rate of return they need to earn. Performance should not be a goal; it's just a way investors can keep score while they work toward their goals.

Fourth, a bear market causes investors to honestly evaluate their abilities to handle their own investments. When the market is soaring and it's hard *not* to make money, investors are lulled into thinking that they can handle their investments. I have seen do-it-yourself investors achieve very attractive returns, too. But a good investor is one who knows how to invest in bull *and* bear markets, and attractive returns are no substitute for solid financial planning. A major correction reminds people that playing the market can be a dangerous game when their retirement is at stake. The market is volatile and fluctuates daily. It's hard to know when to buy or sell, and easy to do both at the wrong times. A financial advisor can explain the market and devise strategies to use to achieve the desired results.

Finally, there's this point from legendary investor Warren Buffett: "Even though there will be net buyers of stocks for many years to come, many investors are elated when stock prices rise and are depressed when they fall. This reaction makes no sense. Only those who will be sellers in the near future should be happy at seeing stocks rise. Prospective purchasers should much prefer sinking prices." Assuming you are a long-term investor, condition yourself to hope for periodic stock market declines. Rather than fear them, view them as necessary, inevitable, and even beneficial, and providing you with opportunities to continue investing.

WON'T I BE HURT BY A BEAR MARKET?

Think of bear markets as periods of time when stocks are returned to their rightful owners. This was reinforced during the summer of 1998. The U.S. stock market did not quite experience a bear market then, but it did have a brief decline of 18 percent over two months. In August of 1998, in the midst of the brief chaos, short-term investors removed $11.3 billion from U.S. stock mutual funds. For the following year and a half, the U.S. stock market performed to the tune of approximately 25 percent, so the $11.3 billion that went into bonds or CDs or under somebody's mattress lost out on serious gains. Investors who stayed the course and invested in equities during the summer of 1998 saw their portfolios grow.

WHY DOES THE STOCK MARKET SOMETIMES DROP WHEN THE U.S. ECONOMY SEEMS TO BE DOING GREAT AND RISE WHEN THE ECONOMY IS IN THE DOLDRUMS?

Throughout history, the stock market has been a forecaster of the future. What I mean by this is that the stock prices you see today reflect what investors feel the stocks will be worth in about 12 to 18 months. So if the market is high and the general consensus is that U.S. corporate profits will erode over the next 12 to 18 months, you will see the stock market correct itself, and vice versa.

Recent history provides us with a good illustration of how the market forecasts the future. In 1991, the U.S. economy was in a recession, but this was a banner year for U.S. stocks. The market and its investors were predicting that corporate America was going to see increased profitability in the following months. Soon enough, the market exploded in a positive direction. So even though Americans felt like we were in a recession in 1991, the S&P 500 surged forward approximately 31 percent.

FEDERAL RESERVE CHAIRMAN ALAN GREENSPAN RAISED INTEREST RATES ONLY TO SEE THE MARKET CLIMB, AND LOWERED INTEREST RATES ONLY TO SEE THE MARKET FALL. SHOULDN'T THE MARKET DROP WHEN INTEREST RATES RISE AND CLIMB WHEN INTEREST RATES FALL?

In the short term, the stock market tries hard to listen to the wisdom of Alan Greenspan, the Chairman of the Federal Reserve Board, because he has been very successful in interpreting the economic data at his disposal. When Mr. Greenspan announces a rate increase or decrease, he also usually provides his sense of the overall health of the economy. For example, when he raised rates in 1999, he implied, to those who were listening, that this very likely was not a serious interest rate hike and that the Board did not foresee another rate increase in the near future. He also implied that he did not believe that in the next 12 to 18 months the economy would be growing too fast, causing interest rates and inflation to rise. All that caused a positive reaction in the stock market. So the markets react not only to the Fed's actions, but also to what Mr. Greenspan has to say about future.

A comment on Mr. Greenspan and the Federal Reserve Board: Please realize that these people do not cause the economy to go into a recession or to overheat. Mr. Greenspan and his colleagues react to the direction of the economy; they don't control it. They react to situations; they don't cause them. To think that the Fed controls the economy is a common misinterpretation of Mr. Greenspan's and the Federal Reserve Board's roles. One final comment: I believe that Mr. Greenspan is worthy of a Nobel Prize in economics, if he qualifies for such an award. At the very least he is going to go down in history as the best Federal Reserve chairman we've ever had.

WHY SHOULDN'T I SELL SOME OF MY LOSING STOCKS WHEN THE MARKET DROPS?

If you look down the road four to five years, what you will find is that corporate profits drive stock prices. As long as a company's earnings are rising, over time its stock price should also rise. If a company's earnings are falling, its stock price should drop.

Unfortunately, in the short term (six months to one year), this is not always the case. In 1994, the stock market earned zero—it did not go up, although corporate profits were up approximately 18 percent. In 1997, the profits of companies in the S&P 500 were up less than 10 percent, but the S&P index, which represents a big chunk of the U.S. stock market, was up 33 percent. You can see that in the short term, there is often no correlation between corporate profits and stock market performance. As an example, Figure 1-1 shows how the earnings from Motorola, Halliburton, Merrill Lynch, and AT&T have tracked their stock prices, respectively, in recent years.

This is why your most successful investors throughout history are long-term investors who focus more on the businesses they own than the market and stock price. This should be you, too. If you are investing for the long term and own solid businesses that are profitable and have potential for future growth, eventually the stock prices will reflect this and rise again.

This approach may sound simple, but it is not easy. Over the course of these four to five years, you will receive monthly or quarterly statements that show that the value of your investment has declined. It will look as if you are losing money. It takes

willpower at such times to think about your investments logi-
cally, and avoid reacting to your emotions and selling when your
stocks are down.

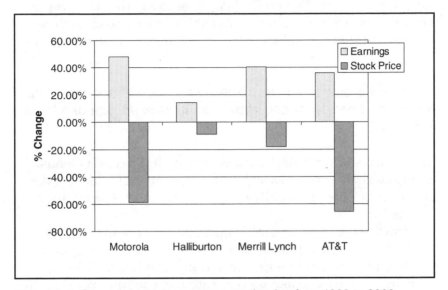

Figure 1-1: Company earnings versus stock price from 1999 to 2000

Recently, a high-school friend called me because he was nervous about the market. He owns stock in the company he works
for because he has faith in the future of the company. However,
the price of his company's stock has been hammered recently, for
many reasons, but mostly due to emotional responses from investors. "Bob, the funny thing is that even though our company's
stock price is down over 30 percent from its high early in the
summer, I'm confident that we are going to hit or exceed our
expectations for profits," he said to me. "We are still making as
much money as we were when the stock was 30 percent higher."
This is a classic example of how the short-term emotional volatility of the stock market differs greatly from the profitability and
growth potential of the companies it is composed of. As we
reviewed the situation, my friend decided not to react to his emotions and instead let the facts dictate his behavior.

WHAT HAPPENS WHEN A COMPANY I USED TO LIKE IS NO LONGER PROFITABLE? WHEN SHOULD I SELL THE STOCK?

One of my heroes, Warren Buffett, likes to say that the proper time to hold a stock is forever. You should buy a stock with the intent that this is a company worth owning for a long, long time.

IF A STOCK IS DOWN, BUT THE COMPANY IS INCREASINGLY PROFITABLE, WHEN WILL I RECEIVE THOSE PROFITS AS A SHAREHOLDER OF THE COMPANY?

If you own stock in a profitable company that pays dividends, then you should receive some of those profits as dividends, the payment of which is usually made quarterly, semi-annually, or annually.

However, if it's a profitable business that doesn't pay dividends but has great prospects for the future, try to be patient. Such companies are like race cars waiting at the starting line: The drivers have one foot on the clutch and another revving the engine. At some point, these companies should be rewarded for the profits they have been achieving, and the price of their stocks should take off in one of two ways: Investors recognize these companies for being great and buy more of the stock, bidding up the price to higher levels, or the companies become candidates to be acquired by other companies at a premium price.

A good example of such a company is Arctic Cat, a producer of jet skis, snowmobiles, and other recreational vehicles. In about May of 1999, you could own this company by paying about $6 for each $1 of profit. This was a great company, with great management that consistently executed its business plan, but hadn't been rewarded for continually achieving its objectives. For some reason, or maybe for no reason at all, the market didn't think this company was worth more than that. However, by 2000, its share price doubled.

Many of the most successful investors—one being Warren Buffett, who may be the most successful investor of the 20th century—pay attention to the actual business that a company is in, whether it has great management and a great brand name, and if it has the capability of executing its business plan. At the same time, if Buffett thinks a company's share price is a good value at

$50, it's an even better value when it drops to $30. You can see that some of your best investments going forward might be of great companies that have not yet been rewarded for executing their business plans!

WHAT IS A P/E RATIO?

A price-to-earnings (P/E) ratio is a company's price per share divided by its earnings per share. For example, if a company's share price is $10 and it earns $1 of profit per share, its P/E ratio is 10. Now, if this same company's earnings grow 30 percent in its next year to $1.30 per share, but its stock price falls from $10 to $7, its P/E ratio falls from 10 all the way down to 5, making it more attractive to value investors.

The P/E ratio provides investors with another data point by which to evaluate stocks. Generally, the stock of a company with a high P/E ratio is more expensive than the stock of a company with a low P/E ratio. By expensive I mean the investor pays more per dollar of profit. Extreme examples of companies with high P/E ratios were the Internet companies. Their high P/E ratios were the result of high stock prices driven by (to borrow a Greenspan phrase) "irrational exuberance" and no profits, making them very expensive buys.

As with anything else, it's important to compare apples to apples. Profits and earnings vary among industries; some are more profitable than others. So it is only meaningful to compare the P/E ratios of companies to others within the same industry, and to the average P/E ratio for that industry.

WHY IS THE DOW JONES INDUSTRIAL AVERAGE CONSIDERED SUCH AN IMPORTANT INDICATOR OF THE STOCK MARKET'S PERFORMANCE?

The reason the Dow Jones Industrial Average (DJIA) is considered an important measure of stock market performance has to do with tradition. In 1884, Charles Henry Dow averaged the closing prices of 11 stocks he considered representative of the U.S. economy, and published the result in a paper that preceded *The Wall Street Journal*. By 1896, *The Wall Street Journal* was publishing this average on a regular basis and the most famous indicator of stock market health—the Dow Jones Industrial Average—was born.

The Dow Jones Industrial Average now monitors the daily change in value of 30 industrial stocks listed on the New York Stock Exchange. All are "blue chip" issues. Many are household names like AT&T, Coca-Cola, Eastman Kodak, IBM, McDonald's, and Disney, and all 30 are considered flagship stocks that serve as an overall representation of the economy and market. The list is very stable, but it has changed over the years.

Of course, the Dow Jones Industrial Average isn't the only market indicator. There are a number of others that provide slightly different information. The Standard & Poor's 500 (S&P 500) is an index based on a group of 500 large stocks, providing a broader picture of the market at any one time, although it doesn't include any mid-sized or small companies. Because some stocks influence the market more than others, each stock is given a different weight when the calculations are made. While the Dow Jones Industrial Average is respected as a traditional way of measuring the stock market's performance, keep in mind that you should follow the stocks you own or are considering buying, and their health is much more important than the Dow or the S&P 500.

I HAVE SEVERAL STOCKS, BUT I DO NOT KNOW ON WHICH STOCK EXCHANGE THEY ARE LISTED. WHAT IS THE BEST AND EASIEST WAY (WITHOUT ASKING MY BROKER) TO FIND OUT ON WHICH EXCHANGES THEY ARE TRADED?

You can look up the companies' names in *Value Line*, a comprehensive research publication that explains many facts about a specific stock issued by a company. Available at many public libraries, the *Value Line* report on each company tells you which stock exchange your stock is traded on—the New York Stock Exchange, American Stock Exchange, or Nasdaq (the over-the-counter stock exchange or automated system).

You can also access this information at *Value Line*'s Web site (www.valueline.com). Under the Markets Center, enter a company's symbol, select "Quote" as your View Options, and click Go. You will be given a list of information about the company, including the exchange on which it's traded. If you don't know the symbol of a company, under the Markets Center, select Symbol Lookup. Type a company's name, click Go, and you'll be given the company's symbol.

This information is also available on other Web sites, such as Yahoo! (www.yahoo.com), as well as in major newspapers, such as *The Washington Post* and *The New York Times*. On Yahoo!, choose Finance, and then Symbol Lookup. Enter the name of the company, and it will give you the exchange on which it's traded.

AFTER ALL THE INTERNET STOCK FRENZY, ARE THE OLD BENCHMARKS STILL USEFUL FOR EVALUATING STOCKS?

There has been some serious discussion about traditional stock market benchmarks and whether they are becoming obsolete. The usefulness of the traditional value benchmarks, such as price-to-earnings (P/E) ratio, cash flow, earnings per share, and others, came into question because many of these indicators had been signaling that stock prices were overvalued, even as stock prices continued to rise. Optimistic analysts contended that stock prices were reasonable because economic conditions, such as low inflation, low interest rates, solid economic growth, rising corporate profits, and strong global trade, were good for common stocks. Others argued that speculative buying inflated stock prices and that today's ideal conditions already are reflected in the prices. Given the way that the Internet group of stocks ended up, with many of them worth pennies if anything at all, it's obvious that the classic investing benchmarks have more staying power than your average dot-com.

SHOULD I BE CONCERNED ABOUT STOCKS THAT SEEM TO BE DOING WELL YET AREN'T PAYING ME VERY MUCH IN DIVIDENDS?

Low dividend yields are not worrisome at all. Interest rates and competing fixed-rate investments, such as CDs, have been relatively low in recent years, so it's not as if stocks are the only category that's not throwing off sizable returns. You should be aware that the tax rate on corporate dividends changed in 2003. To end the double taxation on corporate dividends paid to shareholders, a law was passed that allows for the following: The same 15 percent (or 5 percent for the lowest income tax brackets) maximum tax rate that applies to the net capital gains will be used to calculate taxes owed on dividends. Previous to this change, your dividends were taxed at your ordinary income rate.

Certain dividends from mutual funds, real estate investment trusts, and certain foreign corporations do not qualify for the reduced rate. If a mutual fund is invested in bonds and pays interest, it doesn't qualify. If a mutual fund invests in companies that pay a dividend, that should qualify it for the reduced tax rates.

CAN YOU GIVE ME A GOOD BENCHMARK TO USE TO DETERMINE THE VALUE OF A STOCK?

One very widely used benchmark is called the price-to-book value. This gauge is used to compare the price of a stock to its book value, or the per-share net worth of a company. Net worth is what remains after a company's current bills and longer-term debt are subtracted from its assets (cash, inventory, equipment, buildings, and so on). In the 1990s, the S&P index was trading at more than five times the book value of the underlying shares of stock, more than twice the average over the past twenty years. Another popular measure is the price-to-earnings ratio. P/E ratios will fluctuate based on how the overall market is doing; it is most useful as a comparison between two or three similar stocks you're considering.

SHOULD I BUY THE BEST-PERFORMING STOCK?

It would appear that the obvious answer to this question is yes, but buying stocks that have performed well in the past is exactly what you do not want to do—you want to buy stocks that perform well in the future. If you purchase stocks that have been good performers, you will most likely find that they have high valuations, because "high expectations" have been built into their prices. In other words, you're paying more than the stock may be worth.

Many people enjoy being associated with investments that have been winners in the past, and they choose stocks based on this. To succeed in the stock market, however, you should do the opposite: Invest in stocks that are undervalued and have the potential to be winners in the future. To do this, you must choose your investments objectively, not emotionally. For example, don't buy stock in a company just because your friends own it. Rather, invest in a stock based on the company's merits. Remember, for every successful Pizza Hut there are ten other fast-food chains that looked just as good at the starting gate but finished poorly.

Companies that are universally beloved today tend to carry a unique burden—the expectation of good results! Investors have high expectations of these companies and, therefore, their stock prices do not fluctuate too wildly as long as these companies continue to post good results. However, if there are any negative surprises, Wall Street tends to hammer the prices of these stocks into a downward spiral.

Do yourself a favor when buying stocks or stock mutual funds: Spend time researching so that you find companies whose stock prices have the potential of increasing in the future. Most people, unfortunately, spend their time buying investments that have gone up in the past. This leads to buying high and selling low—a habit you should try to avoid.

CAN YOU GIVE ME AN EXAMPLE OF THE KINDS OF BUSINESS CHARACTERISTICS AND PRACTICES THAT A PROFESSIONAL MANAGER WOULD WANT TO SEE IN A GOOD, STABLE COMPANY?

I once asked a portfolio manager why he was researching a particular company, which I will refer to as XYZ so as not to promote any particular company. He explained to me that with the development of large, multiplex theaters, significant international growth in the entertainment industry, and a large market opportunity, he had begun to research companies in and related to the entertainment industry. He was currently looking at XYZ, because it was the nation's leading producer of commercial feature-film projectors.

What he found in XYZ was a company that had a lot of upside potential. It had what is called sustainable competitive advantages, in that its projectors required a high level of engineering and were also high-quality products. In addition, XYZ was the principal supplier to the leading theater chains.

Perhaps most important, however, was the fact that XYZ had a stable management team and a proven record of success. The management team that was in place at the time had engineered the product development years ago. Another great factor was a large inside ownership: Management and employees owned approximately 13 percent of the outstanding shares through their employee stock option and profit-sharing plans. The company also had a solid financial position: It had no long-term debt and the capability to generate cash flow to fund growth and acquisitions in the future.

IS THERE ANY ONE THING THAT TENDS TO MAKE STOCKS DO WELL?

The factor that positively affects stocks more than any other is growth of earnings. Businesses that increase their earnings year after year have tended to be recognized by investors. After all, who wouldn't want the opportunity to be part owner of a business that had demonstrated its capability to grow?

Let's look at two companies and see how the price of their stocks were affected by earnings. K-Mart's earnings dropped from $2 per share in 1986 to a loss of about 25 cents per share in 1995. Its stock price dropped from about $15 per share in 1986 to somewhere around $7 per share in 1995. K-Mart's price per share over that ten-year period of time was hammered due to lack of earnings growth. On the other hand, Microsoft's earnings grew steadily from about 25 cents per share in 1986 to almost $2.50 per share by the end of 1995, and its stock price steadily climbed from under $1 to over $11 per share. Figure 1-2 shows how K-Mart and Microsoft stocks fared over that time period.

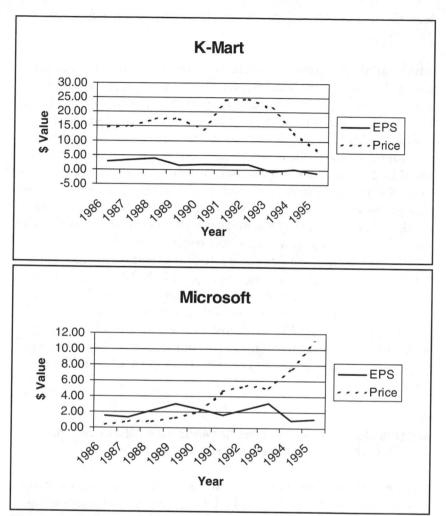

Figure 1-2: K-Mart versus Microsoft

The challenge for most investors is that earnings per share do not grow in lockstep with the stock price. Sometimes, earnings per share is ahead of the stock price and sometimes it's behind. This is a problem for many investors who may consider themselves long-term investors but do not have the patience to allow the businesses to grow their earnings over time.

WHAT IS THE DIFFERENCE BETWEEN A GROWTH STOCK AND A VALUE STOCK?

Investment in a growth stock is an investment in a traditional growth company, such as Dell Computer or Microsoft, whose earnings have grown very fast. Investors generally are willing to pay a high premium for these stocks, because they expect these companies' future earnings to continue to grow at a rapid rate, pushing the stock price even higher. On the other hand, investment in a value stock is an investment in a company whose stock price, for many reasons, is undervalued in the stock market relative to the profit that it is producing. Investors purchase these stocks anticipating that the market will reward these companies down the road, which will increase their stock prices.

Historically, these two categories have complemented each other very well—growth companies tend to be better investments when the economy's going well, and value stocks perform better when it slows down, which is something to keep in mind as you're diversifying your portfolio. Almost every category of investing, whether small companies, large companies, or mid-sized companies, can be broken up into these two categories, growth versus value.

WHAT IS THE DIFFERENCE BETWEEN LARGE-CAPITALIZATION, MID-CAPITALIZATION, AND SMALL-CAPITALIZATION STOCKS?

Capitalization refers to the overall amount of money a company is worth at any given time. It is determined by multiplying the company's outstanding shares of stock by the price per share. The various categories of capitalization indicate the varying levels of growth a company may be in, as well as how much risk may be involved investing in a company. The large-capitalization (or large-cap) category generally consists of companies with values greater than $6 billion. Companies in this category are generally large with recognizable names. They often supply widely used goods and services throughout the global marketplace. They also may be likely to have established histories and are often dominant in their industries. They tend to offer more dependable dividend and return potential, and they are usually categorized as a lower risk investment. However, on the opposite side, there also tends to be less opportunity for outstanding growth down the road.

The mid-capitalization (or mid-cap) category includes companies valued between $2 billion and $6 billion. These are considered mid-sized companies that are well-established in their respective industries but may not be the leaders. They offer some opportunity for growth from expansion, relatively attractive returns, and dividend potential, and they possess attributes that may enable them to assume future leadership in their industry.

The third and final category, small-capitalization (or small-cap), consists of companies with values that are generally under $2 billion. These companies are generally more recently founded, and therefore not as well-established as the others. Smaller companies that are in a constantly evolving industry, such as technology, may also be considered part of this category. They offer greater opportunities for growth as the businesses emerge over the long-term, but they also pose a higher risk since they do not have long records of performance.

WHAT ARE THE PRINCIPAL ADVANTAGES AND DISADVANTAGES TO INVESTING IN SMALL COMPANIES?

A small company with a promising proprietary product or service, or operating in a dynamic field, can have far greater potential for rapid earnings growth than a huge company. Small companies with streamlined management structures should be more flexible than large companies, and better able to seize opportunities and respond to market changes. In addition, their slimmer overhead should enable a larger percentage of rising revenues to flow through to earnings, and more quickly than is usually true of larger companies.

Small companies face disadvantages, too. They have a harder time securing necessary outside financing than larger companies. Their management style may be creative but relatively inexperienced in the rough and tumble of the marketplace. Just as their earnings quickly reflect rising revenues, they will likewise be more sensitive to a setback in sales.

Many small-cap companies are rapidly growing and will turn out to be the investment success stories of tomorrow. Personally, I am more excited about well-managed small-company investments going forward. Since many large companies in the U.S. have downsized, restructured, and therefore outsourced many of their activities, a well-managed small company that can exploit these outsourcing opportunities can really prosper in the future.

In the past, focusing on smaller companies has proven to be one of the best long-term investments you could have made. Since 1925, small-company stocks have outgrown virtually all other types of investments. While these stocks carry a higher degree of risk, over the past thirty years, they have returned, on average, 14.5 percent per year including reinvested dividends. This is nearly double the return on government bonds and Treasury bills. Of course, past performance is not indicative of future results.

I AM A CONSERVATIVE INVESTOR. DOES IT MAKE SENSE TO CONSIDER THE ADDITION OF SMALL-COMPANY INVESTMENTS TO MY PORTFOLIO? INVESTING IN SMALL COMPANIES SEEMS TO BE SO RISKY.

For the patient long-term investor, and even the most conservative one, a diversified, well-managed, small-company portfolio can add financial value to an investor's life. We hear so much about huge multinational corporations, such as McDonald's, AT&T, and IBM that we sometimes underestimate the significance of their smaller counterparts. In fact, nearly 90 percent of publicly traded companies in the United States are considered small companies. These small companies can make significant long-term investments, not only providing strong historical returns, but also achieving those returns from different sources. Therefore, adding smaller companies to a portfolio helps you to diversify while also increasing your long-term potential for appreciation.

Now, I am not recommending that you invest in only a few "hot" stocks or "hot" sectors, because doing this may expose you to excessive and unnecessary risk. What I am recommending is that you look into investing in small-company funds. In effect you are using the services of a professional portfolio manager who shops, extensively researches, and then invests the portfolio in a wide variety of successful fast-growing companies in the small-cap market. This will help you reduce volatility through diversification and help you achieve a more consistent performance over time.

What I can't recommend is what percentage of your portfolio belongs in the small-company investment arena, since I do not know anything about your goals, risk tolerance, investment objectives, time frames, and so on. You should be aware that there are two distinct types of small-company stocks: small-company stocks with growth characteristics and small-company stocks with value characteristics. Small-company growth stocks are frequently the stocks of companies that are expanding their businesses much faster than the average company. These stocks are usually more expensive because investors have already incorporated future growth potential into their current prices. Small-company value stocks, in contrast, are stocks of companies expected to grow at slower, steadier rates and are priced according to the company's current assets, not on their potential for future growth. Because these two distinct types of small companies have performance patterns that differ greatly, a well-diversified portfolio that includes a complement of both growth and value stocks may serve to reduce overall investment risk.

WHAT DOES A PORTFOLIO MANAGER LOOK FOR WHEN EVALUATING A GROWTH STOCK?

There are many things that a fund manager will evaluate when selecting growth stocks for the fund's portfolio. The first is above-average sales and earnings increases. From quarter to quarter and year to year, the company's sales and earnings have grown more than the sales and earnings of their competitors. A second would be price momentum: The stock price has gone up and looks as if it will keep going up, or the price has gone down for a time and looks as if it will go up again. A third attractive characteristic of growth stocks is solid growth potential. The fund manager would look at companies that have strong balance sheets, have seasoned management, and are experiencing rapid growth in new industries or technologies. A fourth would be downside protection. A good portfolio manager will analyze stocks to see how they will perform in down markets as well as up markets.

WHAT DOES A PORTFOLIO MANAGER LOOK FOR WHEN EVALUATING A VALUE STOCK?

The purpose of investing in value stocks is to find stocks that are priced below what the manager thinks they should be. So value managers use a lot of technical analyses to relate a stock to its compatriots in the same industry or that are otherwise similar. A stock with a lower price-to-earnings ratio, lower price-to-book value, and greater earnings per share than a similar stock in the same industry would be very attractive to a value manager.

I AM THINKING ABOUT INVESTING IN STOCKS OF DOMESTIC FOOD COMPANIES, SUCH AS GENERAL MILLS AND COCA-COLA, THAT SELL PRODUCTS WITH GOOD NAME RECOGNITION. DO YOU THINK THIS SIMPLE INVESTMENT STRATEGY CAN BE EFFECTIVE?

Before purchasing stock in some of the more widely known companies that have many products on the retail shelves (other names that come to mind are Wrigley, Quaker Oats, and H.J. Heinz), read the business press to learn about the cultural trends that are affecting these types of companies. For example, American food companies today can no longer depend on rising demand in U.S. markets to propel their growth. The annual growth rate in the U.S. of sales of packaged food has slowed to 1 percent, partly due to the aging population in this country. As people get older, they eat less.

American food companies are fortunate, however, to be operating in an industry that generates a substantial cash flow. Many American companies are tapping that cash flow to implement a variety of strategies to increase their profits. Investing globally is one strategy: In many foreign countries, particularly those in Latin America and the Far East, there are growing numbers of young consumers, and their disposable income is on the rise. Companies such as Coca-Cola and Wrigley began investing in these countries years ago and, because they have had success, continue to do so. Since most local tastes and traditions do not present any resistance to soft drinks and chewing gum, these firms have benefited additionally because of the universal appeal of their mainstay products.

Another profit strategy is through acquisitions. American food companies are using their cash flow to make acquisitions. Those that own products in several different categories often buy out their competitors to increase their corporate profits. H.J. Heinz did this several years ago, when it acquired Quaker Oats' pet-food division. The acquisition enabled H.J. Heinz to cut costs in its pet-food division and increase its share of that market.

IF LARGE COMPANIES DO NOT HAVE THE RESOURCES THAT FOREIGN EXPANSION REQUIRES, AND THEY CANNOT ACQUIRE OTHER COMPANIES BECAUSE THEY OPERATE IN SECTORS WITH JUST A FEW PLAYERS, HOW DO THEY GROW THEIR EARNINGS?

Firms that lack the resources to expand overseas, and cannot use acquisitions as an option, often rely on stock buybacks to increase earnings. Hershey and General Mills are such examples. These firms compete in consolidated categories where only a few players dominate the market and there are few smaller competitors to buy out. Hershey shares the chocolate market with Mars and the Swiss firm Nestlé; General Mills, along with Kellogg and Philip Morris's Post brand name, controls approximately 75 percent of the U.S. cereal market, without any significant smaller competitors. Both Hershey and General Mills have bought back shares of their own company stock to increase earnings. With fewer shares of their stock outstanding in the market, their companies' earnings rose. While this technique brings about earnings growth, international expansion still offers the greatest potential for earnings growth. For this reason, investors are generally willing to pay a higher price for the stocks of the U.S. food companies that are broadening their overseas operations.

I AM NERVOUS ABOUT HAVING MY ASSETS IN JUST A FEW STOCKS. ANY SUGGESTIONS?

I face this issue all the time. My advice is to gradually sell off the stocks, no matter how great the companies are, especially if they've already appreciated in value. Take the federal long-term capital gains tax on the chin, which is 20 percent today, and then protect your assets in a long-term, professionally managed plan that has less vulnerability in the U.S. stock market but allows you to participate in all the great things the stock market has to offer for long-term investors. I know many people who did not sell a large stock holding out of fear of having to pay taxes upon the sale. The result, for many of those people, is that the stock prices dropped and eroded their net worth to the level where it took many years to recover. If they had not focused on the tax implications, but rather weighed the short-term tax payment against the long-term risk of owning only a few stocks, they would have realized the importance of diversifying their portfolios among many long-term, proven asset classes.

YOU RECOMMEND DIVERSIFICATION BY BUYING U.S. AND FOREIGN COMPANIES. MANY COMPANIES ARE BUYING EACH OTHER, HOWEVER. WHEN A U.S. COMPANY AND A FOREIGN COMPANY BECOME ONE, HOW DOES THIS AFFECT MY DIVERSIFICATION?

Mergers and acquisitions are an interesting evolution that is here to stay. As economies continue to globalize and businesses compete with other companies around the world, your investment choices shouldn't be determined by the location of companies' headquarters. The best way to think of this is in terms of investing in U.S. companies. You wouldn't consider your portfolio diversified because you own stock in U.S. companies based in different states. Rather you diversify by investing in small, medium, and large companies, companies in various markets, and the like.

If you are trying to achieve true diversification through asset allocation (for a discussion of asset allocation, see Section 4, "Investing"), you should focus more on industry diversification. If a health-care or pharmaceutical stock drops, it's possible that other stocks—and maybe even the sector—will be negatively affected. It's not going to matter where the companies are based. Therefore, owning non-U.S. pharmaceutical companies and U.S. pharmaceutical companies does not add much diversification to your portfolio. Rather, Germany-based Bayer should be analyzed side by side with U.S.-based Pfizer. Diversifying and weighting your portfolio based on industry and sectors is going to be paramount.

ARE THERE ANY ADVANTAGES TO OWNING PREFERRED STOCK OVER COMMON STOCK?

There are some distinct advantages to investing in preferred stock over common stock. Preferred stock gets its name from two ways in which it has preference over common stock. First, a corporation must pay dividends to its preferred shareholders before it can pay any dividends to its common stock holders. Second, in the event that the corporation files for bankruptcy, the preferred shareholder's claims on the corporation's assets are considered before the claims of the common stockholders.

Although preferred stock is categorized as an equity security, it has features that are similar to both common stocks and bonds (debt securities). Like common stock, shares of preferred stock represent shares of ownership in the corporation, and preferred stock owners have the right to receive dividends. However, the owners of preferred stock are more like silent owners. Unlike common stockholders, owners of preferred stock typically have no voting rights and, therefore, no voice in the management of the corporation. Dividends, which must be declared by the company, are usually paid quarterly. However, the percentage or amount of dividends each preferred share receives is fixed when the security is issued to the public. The dividend payments will remain the same for as long as the security is outstanding. In this way, a preferred stock is like a bond on which the interest rate is set at the time the security is issued and remains the same throughout its life. Unlike a bond, however, a preferred stock share does not have a maturity date; it has an indefinite life. The greatest advantage the preferred stockholder would have over common stock owners would be the presumably higher level of income the preferred stockholder would receive.

WHEN THE STOCK MARKET OVERHEATS, MANY PEOPLE STILL BUY STOCKS. HOW DO THEY JUSTIFY THIS?

When you say overheat, I assume you mean when prices for U.S. stocks are exorbitant. When I talk to portfolio managers with proven track records, I find that they still can locate great companies at good values in an overpriced environment. First, they focus on companies with expected earnings growth potential of

12–15 percent, even though the economy is growing in the 2–3 percent range. Second, they look for companies that have predictable earnings rather than volatile earnings and whether or not these companies can continue to support the growth expected in their earnings.

Third, and very importantly, they look at the quality of the management in the companies. Fourth, they look for a company with high cash flow and financial flexibility in the marketplace. That means that the company has enough money to invest in plants, equipment, and the like, and can take its excess cash flow and reinvest it into better products and services. And finally, they look to ensure that the valuations of these companies, after the analyses are performed, are reasonable so that the investor is not overpaying for the ownership of a company. There always will be sections of the market that are overheating, and sections of the market that hold good values.

WHAT DO YOU FEEL THE FUTURE HOLDS FOR THE MARKETS?

Looking forward, I am very excited about the future of the investment markets both in the U.S. and abroad. That is not to say that the market only will go up in the future. I believe it will go up, but we will continue to see fluctuating markets and bear markets as well. What makes me optimistic is that, historically, bear markets have been very short lived. Since 1953, the S&P 500 has declined 15 percent or more fourteen times. The average decline has lasted eight months, and 75 percent of the loss was recouped within seven months. On average, a full market rebound took just over a year, and the rallies that have followed bear markets have been strong. For example, stock prices rose 42 percent in the three months of the bull market that started in 1982. From 1963 through 1993, stock investors who were out of the market for the best 90 trading days missed 95 percent of the market's gains.

On July 8, 1932, the Dow Jones Industrial Average reached an intraday low of 40. During the boom of the late 1990s, it reached over 11,500. If our financial system has taught us one thing, it is faith. We can't begin to count the number of times the market has gone down—the key is that it has never stayed down.

SECTION 2

~

BONDS

7 THINGS YOU SHOULD KNOW ABOUT BONDS

➢ Bonds are more stable investments than stocks

➢ Bonds are not risk-free

➢ Buy bonds to protect principal or produce income

➢ Diversify—this doesn't apply only to stocks

➢ Buy bonds based on the future quality of the lender

➢ Hold bonds until maturity and price fluctuations won't matter

➢ A bond investor's worst enemy is inflation or rising prices

B onds are a form of debt. The company or governmental entity that issues a bond needs a loan, and agrees to pay interest on a set schedule and repay the principal amount on a stated maturity date. Corporate bonds offer investors a higher degree of safety than most stocks since they rank senior to both common and preferred stocks. In other words, if the corporation that issued the bonds were to be liquidated, the bondholders would be paid before the stockholders. Government bonds, which include U.S. Treasuries, municipal bonds, foreign bonds, and various other categories, offer a higher degree of safety than corporate bonds—governments go bankrupt less often than companies do—but also generally offer lower returns.

In general, here's how bonds work: Let's say you buy a ten-year bond with a face value of $10,000 and a 7 percent coupon rate (or interest rate). You, in essence, are a lender and are lending the issuer of the bond $10,000 with the understanding that it will pay you a coupon rate of 7 percent per year, usually in semi-annual installments, until the bond matures. For the next ten years, assuming you don't sell the bond in the meantime, you will receive two $350 payments each year, or $700 annually. When the bond matures, your $10,000 principal will be repaid.

If you keep your bond until it matures, changes in the bond's price result in nothing more than paper losses or paper gains. However, many investors do not hold their bonds until maturity. Millions of dollars of outstanding bonds are traded every day on the secondary market, because their total expected yields vary with fluctuations in interest rates.

Let's say you buy a $1,000 Stop & Shop bond that pays you 7 percent interest for 10 years. If you own your bond until maturity, you'll be repaid your $1,000 after collecting your 7 percent or $70 per year in interest. A year after you purchase your bond, however, interest rates increase, and a national food chain similar to Stop & Shop issues an 11 percent interest-bearing bond. Your Stop & Shop bond would most likely be worth less than $1,000 if you wanted to sell it. Why? Because investors won't pay $1,000 for a bond with a 7 percent coupon rate when they can get a comparable bond with an 11 percent rate. Therefore, if you sold your bond, it would be sold at a discount. If, however, comparable bonds had a coupon rate of 6 percent, then you could sell your bond for more than $1,000.

When interest rates are rising and outstanding bonds are selling at a discount, a bond's current yield will be higher than its coupon rate. For example, if interest rates were higher than 7 percent, that $10,000 bond we were discussing might be selling for $9,000, so it would have a current yield of 7.78 percent ($700/$9,000 = 7.78 percent). The reverse is true when interest rates are falling. If that $10,000 bond were selling for $11,000 because of a decrease in interest rates, it would have a current yield of 6.36 percent ($700/$11,000 = 6.36 percent). So depending on whether you want the increase in income or the overall increase in value, you'd either buy or sell that bond.

I HAVE OWNED A BOND FOR OVER A YEAR AND THE PRICE HAS ACTUALLY GONE DOWN A FEW CENTS. SHOULD I CONTINUE TO HOLD ONTO AN INVESTMENT LIKE THIS?

Let me answer this with an example. I have owned a particular bond since 1987, which I bought after that year's stock market crash. This bond was introduced to new investors at $100 per unit. In 1997, the price was $98.874. Ten years passed and the price had gone down by a dollar and 12.6 cents. Many people perceive a bond to be similar to a stock investment and, therefore, wonder why anyone would own an investment whose price has not increased in ten years. But this question is based on a misconception of how bonds really work. For a good quality bond to stay at or even dip below its original price is normal. It fluctuates from day to day, but a bond's price rarely appreciates considerably.

Rather than price changes, focus on the interest rate (or coupon rate) you are receiving, the quality rating on the bond, and the duration of the bond. Bonds are conservative investments that should be used to protect principal or produce income. For this reason bond investors should hope the price does not fluctuate.

The only time the price per share will come into play is if you want to sell the bond. That is because you would be selling your bond at the current trading price, which could be slightly higher or lower than when you bought it. Until you are actually ready to sell your investment, keep focusing on the accumulation of the interest.

WHY DO BONDS PERFORM BETTER WHEN THE ECONOMY IS EXPECTED TO SLOW DOWN?

Not every type of bond performs better when the economy is expected to slow down, although U.S. government bonds and tax-free municipal bonds usually do. One type of bond that does not perform well in a recessionary environment is high-yield corporate bonds, otherwise known as junk bonds.

The greatest fears of most bond investors is inflation and the prospect of inflation. Inflation erodes the real return on a bond, because the amount of interest you receive stays the same for the term of the bond even if inflation rises. The prospect of inflation can erode the price of a bond, because inflation causes interest rates to rise which, in turn, pushes bond prices down. Such price devaluations only affect those selling bonds before their maturity dates, but this is what the bond market does every day. So you can see why even the prospect of inflation is troubling to bond investors. Inflation erodes the returns on your stocks as well, but the price of those stocks is likely to increase in times of an over-heating economy.

When the growth of the economy is expected to slow, normally inflation also slows. Since a bond investor's worst fear is inflation, the bond market welcomes a slowing economy. I like to say that the only thing a bond investor loves more than a slowing economy is a recession.

Bonds also perform better in economic slowdowns because of the influx of capital. A sell-off of equities or stocks usually accompanies a slowing economy. That cash normally is invested in other types of investment vehicles. People looking for safe havens often turn to bonds, which can cause a flood of cash into the bond market. If a lot of new cash comes chasing the same supply of government bonds, however, based on the theory of supply and demand, the prices of the bonds rise and the interest rates fall.

WHY ARE MY BOND FUNDS DECLINING WHEN THE STOCK MARKET IS FALLING? I THOUGHT BONDS WOULD HELP PROTECT MY ASSETS IN A SLOW ECONOMY.

Although it's usually a safe bet to assume that bonds will protect against a market correction, it's difficult to generalize about bonds and stocks. In 1994, when the stock market earned a zero rate of return for investors, U.S. government and municipal investments did poorly, but those notorious junk bonds did well. In each business cycle certain investments pull more of their weight than others, some do not pull any of their weight, and some act just as they are supposed to act. I can only assume that if your bond funds have been going down along with your stock funds, you must have some high-yield bonds or foreign bonds in your portfolio.

THE PRICE OF MY BONDS KEEPS GOING DOWN. HOW MUCH VALUE CAN THEY LOSE BEFORE I'M IN TROUBLE AND SHOULD SELL?

If you or your broker believe that you own bonds of good-quality entities that are not in jeopardy of going bankrupt, and you plan to hold the bonds until maturity, then you should keep the bonds even if they continue to lose value. Upon maturity, you should receive your original principal back regardless of how much value erodes between now and the maturity date. It is important to remember that your income from a bond stays the same even if the price goes down.

Even if the bond issuer does go bankrupt, you may not be left with nothing. Back in the 1980s, when the City of Bridgeport, Connecticut, claimed bankruptcy and defaulted on its bonds, the bonds still had a value of 60 to 70 cents on the dollar. Investors could have sold their bonds and reclaimed a significant portion of their original principal.

HOW DO CORPORATE BONDS DIFFER FROM GOVERNMENT BONDS?

Corporations issue bonds to finance capital improvements or to reduce their reliance on bank financing. Or they may issue them simply to provide working capital for the corporation. The income that you, as an investor, derive from these bonds is fully taxable, unlike some government bonds. In addition, these bonds are not insured and are backed only by the corporation's ability to pay, which depends on the corporation's ability to generate sufficient cash flow after expenses and taxes to repay its debt.

Government bonds are issued by public entities including states, cities, and counties, as well as school districts, development authorities, hospitals, and other nonprofits. Public entities derive their income from taxes, assessments, or the monies generated by these public works. Bonds issued specifically by governments are often free from federal income tax, and some are even double tax-free, incurring no federal or local tax. It takes a spectacular case, such as the Orange County bankruptcy a few years back, for a top-rated government bond to fail to repay its debt.

HOW DO BOND RATINGS WORK?

Corporate and municipal bonds are rated by services such as Moody's Investors Service and Standard & Poor's. The ratings are designed to provide investors with a simple way of selecting bonds according to the level of credit risk, or the ability of the bond's issuer to pay back the principal and interest on the money borrowed.

The two rating firms use similar symbols to indicate gradations of quality: Aaa, Aa, A, Bbb, Bb, B, Ccc, Cc, C, D. (These ratings are pronounced triple A, double A, single A, and so on.) Both of these agencies rate bonds in order of the perceived chances of default, which is when an issuer fails on its promise to pay coupon interest or to pay principal at the agreed-upon time. Studies show a high correlation between credit ratings and actual default experience. The four top categories—AAA/Aaa, AA/Aa, A/A and BBB/Baa—are referred to as investment-grade bonds, while bonds with lower ratings are considered speculative. Table 2-1 shows all the bond ratings and how they're defined.

You may wonder why anyone would buy a bond rated any lower than AAA/Aaa. Usually, lower-rated bonds pay higher rates of interest to make them more attractive to purchasers. Unrated bonds, some of which are held by bond funds, do not necessarily lack quality. It could be that the corporation or governmental units that issued them did not apply for ratings for one reason or another.

Table 2-1: Ratings Index

Investment Grade								
Moody's Aaa	Aa1	Aa2	Aa3	A1	A2	A3	Baa1	Baa2
S&P AAA	AA+	AA	AA-	A+	A	A-	BBB+	BBB

Sub-Investment Grade									
Moody's Ba1	Ba2	Ba3	B1	B2	B2	B3	Caa1	Caa2	Caa3
S&P BB+	BB	BB-	B+	B2	B-	CCC+	CCC	CCC-	CC

With respect to ratings from Standard & Poor's: "+" means rating may be raised; "-" means rating may be lowered.

For Bond Funds Specifically:

AAAf   The fund's portfolio holdings provide extremely strong protection against losses from credit defaults.

Aaf   The fund's portfolio holdings provide very strong protection against losses from credit defaults.

Af   The fund's portfolio holdings provide strong protection against losses from credit defaults.

BBBf   The fund's portfolio holdings provide adequate protection against losses from credit defaults.

BBf   The fund's portfolio holdings provide uncertain protection against losses from credit defaults.

Bf   The fund's portfolio holdings exhibit vulnerability to losses from credit defaults.

CCCf   The fund's portfolio holdings make it extremely vulnerable to losses from credit defaults.

WHAT ARE JUNK BONDS?

Generally, bonds provide a high degree of security, but their yields are often disappointing or even negative after you factor in income taxes and the erosion due to inflation. That is why many fixed-income investors—investors seeking a guaranteed, steady return—like the total return potential offered by high-yield bonds, which the media have termed junk bonds.

High-yield bonds are bonds issued by corporations that have received low credit ratings from the rating agencies, because the agencies perceive a risk in the issuer's ability to repay its debt. In order to attract investors to buy their bonds despite their poor ratings, these companies offer investors a high yield. Therefore, these bonds offer higher income potential for those investors who are willing to accept more risk and are able to stomach fluctuation.

The issuers of high-yield bonds are often familiar companies that provide everyday products and services. For example, Time Warner, United Airlines, Turner Broadcasting Systems, Stop & Shop, Fruit of the Loom, Staples, and Revlon are all companies whose credit ratings were poor when they needed extra capital and, therefore, issued junk bonds to finance their business needs, such as equipment, product enhancement, and research. While these companies weren't seen as having high credit worthiness, this did not necessarily make them weak companies. They simply had more debt than the average company.

HOW RISKY IS IT TO INVEST IN HIGH-YIELD BONDS?

There are several myths surrounding high-yield bonds. One is that they are more volatile than stocks. From 1985 to 1995, the average return for 30-year U.S. Treasury bonds was 9.3 percent per year, the average return for high-yield bonds was 11.8 percent per year, and the average return for U.S. stocks was 14.9 percent per year. In these ten years, high-yield bonds delivered 79 percent of the return of stocks; however, according to the formulas used by analysts who measure such things, they did so with only 47 percent of the volatility. Part of the reason for this is because the value of high-yield securities is tied less to interest rate changes and more to the financial strength of the company issuing the bonds.

A second myth is that high-yield bonds are the creation of greedy, corporate raiders. The reality is that high-yield bonds are often issued by small- to medium-sized companies to finance improvement and business expansion. A third myth is that high-yield bond mutual funds are not liquid and could tie up an investor's money. The reality is that if you invest in a professionally managed mutual fund, your money is easily accessible whenever you need it.

The last myth about high-yield bonds is that many of these bonds default and people lose their entire investments. In reality, on average, less than 3 percent of all high-yield bonds have defaulted each year, and even in those situations, the investors have recovered about forty cents on their investment dollar. For example, the percentage of high-yield bonds that went into default in November of 1995 was 3.26 percent; the rate of defaults in August of 1996 was 2.2 percent, or an average of 2.73 percent.

Over time, as the companies that issue high-yield bonds continue to grow and become more successful, the interest rates you will be able to earn on those bonds will decline. This means that the spread between less risky bonds and high-yield bonds will narrow, and the potential rewards you will receive for owning high-yield bonds and taking more risk will diminish.

WHAT ARE THE ADVANTAGES TO INVESTING IN A HIGH-YIELD BOND FUND?

If you have neither the time nor the inclination to follow the bond market, hiring a professional to manage a basket of high-yield bonds in a mutual fund makes a lot of sense. They will ensure you have the necessary ingredients for success.

Broad diversification is one essential ingredient for success in the high-yield market. One well-managed high-yield bond fund that I follow is diversified among 145 carefully selected issues of 123 companies, spread across 22 industries. An active professional management team can carefully screen and select various bond issues, and maintain a broadly diversified portfolio.

Another essential ingredient needed to achieve success in the high-yield bond market is thorough, ongoing credit analysis, including screening individual issues and tracking industry and economic trends. Investing in high-yield bonds is a long-term process. A high-caliber management team has the knowledge and resources to interpret this information, identify and make sound judgments about tomorrow's opportunities, and react quickly to changes in the high-yield market.

WHAT ARE GOVERNMENT SECURITIES INVESTMENTS?

Government securities investments, which are very popular with conservative investors, include Treasury bills (or T-bills), notes, and bonds. The different names refer to the life span of the various Treasuries: T-bills have a maturity of less than a year, notes have a maturity of from one to ten years, and bonds have a maturity of more than ten years. Government securities investments also include mortgage-backed securities. Debt obligations, such as Treasuries, are issued by the U.S. government to finance government expenditures.

WHAT AFFECTS MY REAL RETURN ON TREASURY BONDS?

Inflation, which I call the invisible tax, affects your return the most. As a U.S. government bond investor, you are lending your money to the U.S. government for a fixed, guaranteed interest rate. You typically collect your interest semi-annually and, at the end of a period of time, you get back your money. However, if inflation rises or falls during this period, while your interest payment remains the same, your real return will be affected. Let's look at an example.

You decide to buy a $5,000 Treasury bond at a 5 percent interest rate. Going forward on a semi-annual basis, then, you receive $125 in interest payments, or $250 annually. If you are in the 35 percent tax bracket, $87.50 of this will go toward taxes, leaving you with $162.50. But this is not your real return.

If you bought the bond when inflation was 3 percent, your real return would be $12.50. (Multiply $5,000 by 3 percent, and subtract the result of $150 from $162.50.) However, if while you own the bond, inflation rises to 4 percent, your real return becomes negative: -$37.50. Conversely, if inflation falls to 2 percent, your real return becomes $62.50.

As you can see, the most opportune time to invest in government securities is when the gap between current interest rates and the current inflation level is wide. In 1979, when inflation levels were at 13 percent, government bonds had yields at around the same levels. Investors in these instruments had negative returns after paying income tax on the earned interest. As inflation dropped in subsequent years, however, government bonds produced positive returns for their investors.

There is now over $6 trillion invested in government securities, which represents around $24,000 for every man, woman, and child in the U.S. Investment vehicles comprised solely of these securities are viewed as having a high degree of safety. Investors seeking better returns than may be available in traditional banking instruments, such as CDs and money market accounts, may want to consider government securities investments.

WHAT IS A MORTGAGE-BACKED INVESTMENT?

The most common mortgage-backed investment is a pool of securities that is made up of the mortgages of individual homeowners. Homeowners take out mortgages with banks and—often instantaneously—the banks sell these mortgages to various government agencies. Some of the agencies that purchase these mortgages are the Government National Mortgage Association (Ginnie Mae), the Federal Home Loan Mortgage Corporation (Freddie Mac), and the Federal National Mortgage Association (Fannie Mae).

Each agency puts together the mortgages it has purchased and sells them to investors in the form of bonds. The interest payments received from the mortgage holders are pooled by the agencies and paid out to the agencies' bondholders. It is the bondholders, the people who invest in the issues of these agencies, who supply the money to create these mortgages. Investors infuse the agencies with money, thus providing them with the capital to purchase the mortgages from banks. Once banks have sold their mortgages and recouped their investments, they have money to make additional construction and mortgage loans. Since the interest and principal are passed through these agencies, these bonds are commonly referred to as pass-through certificates. Figure 2-1 illustrates how money passes from homeowners to bondholders.

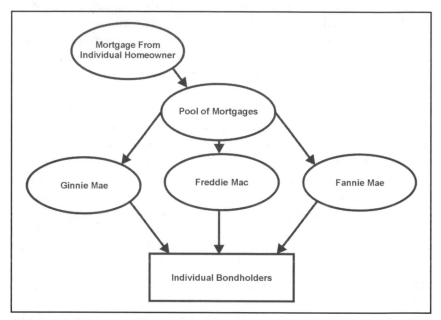

Figure 2-1: Mortgage-backed investments

While the agencies guarantee prompt payment of principal and interest on their bonds, the pooled mortgages are insured by various federal agencies. Mortgages backed by the federal government can be insured by the Veterans Administration (VA) or guaranteed by either the Federal Housing Authority (FHA) or the Farmers Home Administration (FmHA).

The risks associated with mortgage funds are called prepayment risks. In essence, as mortgage rates decline, homeowners who took out mortgages may refinance and secure a lower rate mortgage on their homes. That chunk of money in the mortgage pool is then prepaid. Although mortgage-backed investments seek a stable share price, the share prices will fluctuate, so that when the shares are redeemed they may be worth more or less than the original cost.

ON OCCASION, TWO- AND FIVE-YEAR TREASURY NOTES PAY HIGHER INTEREST THAN TWENTY- AND THIRTY-YEAR TREASURY BONDS. I THOUGHT THAT THE LONGER YOU LEND MONEY TO THE GOVERNMENT, THE HIGHER THE INTEREST YOU RECEIVE. WHY DOES THIS HAPPEN?

This phenomenon is called an inverted yield curve, and occurs at certain times in an economic cycle when short-term interest rates are higher than long-term interest rates. This unusual dynamic usually occurs when the economy is growing in an accelerated fashion. The inverted yield curve is illustrated in Figure 2-2. Contrast this to the normal yield curve shown in Figure 2-3.

I will use an example to explain why this inverted yield curve occurs. If you own a shoe store and the economy is roaring, people are buying your shoes like gangbusters. Because you keep turning over your inventory, it needs replenishing in a more rapid fashion than you're used to. Many small business owners borrow money short-term to finance the replenishing of their inventory. If you compound that on a nationwide scale, in an accelerated economy, you have more people borrowing money on a short-term basis than on a long-term basis.

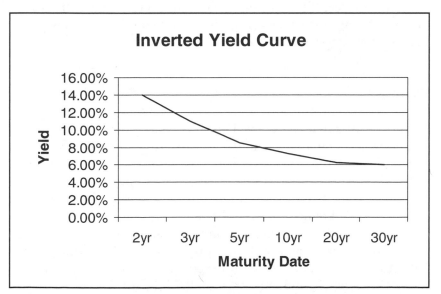

Figure 2-2: Inverted yield curve (For illustration only; numbers are not from any particular source.)

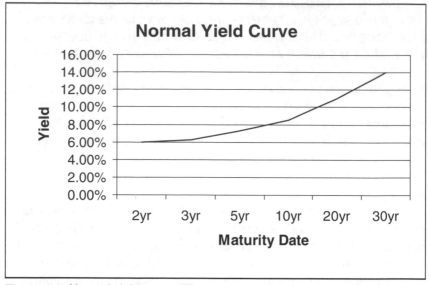

Figure 2-3: Normal yield curve (For illustration only; numbers are not from any particular source.)

Because of this accelerated demand for short-term money, short-term borrowing rates are pushed higher than long-term borrowing rates. If the economy slows down or there is an acceleration of long-term borrowing, then the inverted yield curve returns to normalcy.

WHAT ARE TAX-FREE MUNICIPAL BONDS?

Tax-free municipal bonds are long-term debt securities that are issued by municipalities and are exempt from federal income taxes. If you purchase bonds issued by municipalities of the state in which you are a legal resident, you are exempt from paying state as well as federal income tax on the interest. These bonds are often called double tax-free bonds.

To encourage investment in public entities, such as the city of Hartford in Connecticut or the Tappan Zee Bridge Authority in New York, municipalities not only pay investors interest, but using this type of bond, ensure that the interest they earn is tax-free. The interest paid on tax-free investments is generally lower, however, than the interest paid on taxable investments.

How can I determine if I should be invested in tax-free or taxable bonds?

Assuming that bonds belong in your portfolio, there are three main things to establish that, in turn, will help you determine which bonds are for you. First, you should determine your return from each investment; that is, how much money you will earn after taxes. To do this, you'll need to know your tax bracket, which ranges from 15 percent to 39.6 percent. For a taxable bond, calculate the interest you would receive each year. Then, multiply the annual interest payment by your tax bracket. The result is the amount you will owe in state and federal taxes. Subtract this figure from the annual interest payment and the result is the amount you will keep after taxes.

For the tax-free bond, determine if state taxes are owed. If so, determine the tax rate and multiply the annual interest payment by this rate. This is the amount of state taxes you will owe. Subtract this figure from the annual interest payment you will receive. The result is the amount that will go into your pocket after taxes.

After following these steps, you are comparing apples to apples—the after-tax income from each investment.

Second, you should evaluate the risk associated with these bonds and determine your risk tolerance level. Many companies, such as Moody's Investors Service and S&P, rate bonds, so determining a bond's risk is usually easier than establishing your risk tolerance. For a discussion on how to determine your risk tolerance, see Section 4, "Investing."

Tax-free bonds are attractive in certain markets even for people in low tax brackets. Believe it or not, often there is a very small difference in what can be earned in a high-quality taxable investment versus a high-quality tax-free investment. So why would an investor purchase a high-quality taxable investment when he or she can get the same interest rate in a high-quality tax-free investment? While there are some differences that would cause an investor to choose taxable over tax-free, more likely than not, he or she simply did not figure out which investment returns more after-tax income.

Third, you should determine what I call total return. In many bond investments you have the ability, through good research and a disciplined selection process, to purchase bonds that not only offer interest but the potential for capital appreciation. Successful bond investors do not focus on interest alone, but total return. This usually means that they purchase bonds that have lower interest rates but more capital appreciation potential. Most investors chase high interest rates, and this is where they go wrong. They do not realize that an approach that works for some investments, such as CDs, is not the right approach for other types of investments. In most cases with bond investing, tax-free or taxable, this is not the best approach to take.

One last bit of advice: Do yourself a favor and don't get overly excited about the sexiness of tax-free bonds. Although they are very attractive and a very good investment class, there are differences in these bonds, and they may not be for everybody.

I OWN TAX-FREE BONDS AND HAVE SOLD SEVERAL OF THEM FOR MORE THAN WHAT I PAID. MY FRIEND THINKS I HAVE TO PAY TAXES ON THE PROFIT, BUT I DISAGREE BECAUSE THEY ARE TAX-FREE BONDS. CAN YOU SETTLE THIS ONE FOR US?

The interest that we earn from loaning the government our money is tax-free for federal—and sometimes state—income tax purposes. However, if you lend a city government $10,000, and one year later you sell that bond for $11,000, you did sell an asset for a profit—even though it is a tax-free municipal bond. For tax purposes you will owe a maximum of 20 percent capital gains tax on that $1,000 profit, or approximately $200, to the federal government. The tax-free aspect of the bond is the interest or the income stream. Your friend is correct in this situation—you will have to pay taxes on the profit from selling the bonds.

AS A CONNECTICUT RESIDENT, I'M LOOKING AT SOME LONG-TERM CONNECTICUT DOUBLE TAX-FREE BONDS, YIELDING ABOUT 4 PERCENT INTEREST. WHAT DO YOU THINK?

As an investor, you are better off purchasing or owning tax-free bonds predominately outside the state of Connecticut. I say this for two reasons. First, you can buy tax-free bonds outside Connecticut that would let you keep more of the return. For example, if you buy a tax-free bond anywhere within the U.S. (except Connecticut) or Puerto Rico at an interest rate higher than 4 percent—let's say 4.8 percent—and pay the Connecticut state or any applicable local tax, the remainder is approximately 4.6 percent. This 4.6 percent is your return, because it's tax-free on a federal level, and it's better than the 4 percent you would have earned buying double tax-free Connecticut bonds.

Second, bonds for other areas of the U.S. could offer you appreciation on your investment in addition to interest. Many states are growing faster than Connecticut, which can translate to more tax revenue for the municipalities to which you are lending your money. So I would suggest that you not only focus on the interest that the tax-free bonds produce, but on the potential for appreciation of capital.

WHAT IS THE DIFFERENCE BETWEEN REVENUE OBLIGATION BONDS AND GENERAL OBLIGATION BONDS?

Revenue obligation bonds are municipal bonds whose interest payments generally depend upon the future revenue of the project that they are financing, which makes them riskier than general obligation bonds. If the revenue doesn't come through, or if there are cost overruns on the project the bonds are paying for, the entity might have trouble meeting its obligations. General obligation bonds are backed by the issuer's pledge of its full faith, credit, and taxing power for the payment of principal and interest.

Here are two examples: A town's water department can issue revenue obligation bonds that will be paid for by people buying water; a school district, on the other hand, offers general obligation bonds since its sole source of revenue is the tax base.

If the bonds are to finance a project that won't bring in any revenue for some time—let's say the town needs to build a new water treatment plant—they can be what's called capitalized interest bonds. These bonds don't pay any interest for the first, say, two or three years, until the revenue starts coming in. Obviously, they will likely have a larger payoff in the end.

WHAT IS MUNICIPAL BOND INSURANCE?

Municipal bond insurance is a guarantee by a financial guarantee company that it will make principal and interest payments
on time and in full to the bondholders in the event of a default by
the issuer. Municipal bond insurance may cover new issues,
bonds traded in the secondary market, and those held in mutual
funds. All municipal bonds that are insured by a top-flight bond
insurer, such as MBIA or FGIC, are automatically rated AAA by
Moody's Investors Service and Standard & Poor's. There are
insurers who bring lower-rated bonds up to the AA or A levels as
well. Although there have been a few defaults on insured municipal bonds, my philosophy is that the only municipal bonds that
agencies will generally insure are typically municipal bonds that
do not need insurance.

HISTORICALLY, HAS THERE EVER BEEN AN INSTANCE WHEN AN INSURED MUNICIPAL BOND FAILED TO PAY EITHER INTEREST OR PRINCIPAL?

No, there has never been one case where a financial guarantee
company failed to pay interest and principal on a defaulted
municipal bond. An example of the protection provided by municipal bond insurance involves the largest default in municipal
bond history—the $2.3 billion Washington Public Power Supply
System revenue bonds, which defaulted back in 1983. Some $2.3
million of these revenue bonds were insured by a guarantor. The
investors who owned the insured bonds continued to receive all of
their interest and principal payments as scheduled. On the other
hand, all the owners of the uninsured WPPSS revenue bonds
became embroiled in long and costly litigation, and recovered
only a portion of their original investments. In the history of the
financial guarantee business, no investor has ever failed to
receive timely principal and interest payments when an insured
municipal bond defaulted.

WHAT HAPPENED TO THE INSURED ORANGE COUNTY BONDS WHEN THE COUNTY FILED FOR BANKRUPTCY?

While uninsured Orange County bonds were quickly downgraded to a low investment grade, otherwise known as junk, the insured Orange County bonds retained their AAA rating because of the financial strength of the bond insurance companies. Late in October 1994, before the news of the county's financial difficulties broke, both insured and uninsured Orange County Transportation Authority bonds of the same maturity had comparable yield and prices. Following the county's bankruptcy filing, according to the valuation by the Orange County Transportation Authority, the uninsured bonds were priced 13 percent lower than the insured bonds.

WHAT ARE CONVERTIBLE BONDS AND WHY WOULD I CONSIDER OWNING THEM?

Convertible securities, which can be either bonds or preferred stock, can be converted into (or exchanged for) the issuer's common stock at a predetermined price. A convertible bond investor gets the growth potential associated with the underlying stocks plus the income and downside protection offered by the bonds.

Most people are attracted to what I call all-weather investments—investments that are suited for a variety of different market conditions. Because economies run in cycles, most investments experience periods of strong or weak performance. The convertible security is one investment class that offers all-weather potential. In an expanding economy, if the issuer's stock goes up, holders of these securities can benefit by exchanging them for stock and eventually selling them. In a contracting economy, convertible bonds and preferred stock act as a cushion because they pay a fixed rate of interest or dividend.

Additionally, convertible bonds provide some downside protection because, unlike common stock, convertibles can fall only to the level of their value as income-producing investments. Even though convertibles may entail more risk than normal bonds, they have historically outperformed most other types of fixed-income securities.

WHAT IS A ZERO-COUPON BOND?

Zero-coupon bonds, commonly known as zeros, are primarily issued by the U.S. Treasury, although other governmental entities may issue them as well. The difference between zeros and conventional interest-paying bonds is that zeros pay all interest and principal on the maturity date.

For example, you might be able to purchase a ten-year, zero-coupon security that has a maturity value of $10,000 with only a $5,000 initial investment. During the ten-year period, interest would accrue, but you would not receive it. Rather, at the end of the ten-year period, you would be paid $10,000. Yields vary, but on average they're modestly higher than equivalent regular U.S. government bonds.

Zero-coupon securities have increased in popularity with fixed-income investors. By foregoing the traditional current income stream, these securities allow investors to realize substantial growth of capital. This makes them a good investment when tailoring a financial plan to help meet specific future needs. Zeros are popular with investors who wish to avoid the risk of having to reinvest money in another instrument and who want a specific sum of money to be available on a certain date in the future. This is why they have been popular college planning vehicles. Many parents who are planning ahead to finance a child's college education will purchase zero-coupon bonds that will mature around the time that the child is ready for college.

Zero-coupon securities are also very marketable. This means you can sell your bond before maturity at the current market value if you do need to liquidate. However, these securities are more volatile than traditional fixed-income securities. During a rising interest rate environment, the market value of the zeros may decline. The reverse is also true. During a period of declining interest rates, this volatility can be a considerable advantage.

ARE THERE ANY TAX IMPLICATIONS TO ZERO-COUPON BONDS?

As a matter of fact, one aspect of zero-coupon bonds that many people are not aware of is that even though you don't receive cash returns until well in the future when the bond matures, you do get a 1099 every year for tax purposes. So you must pay taxes on the interest as it is earned, even though you don't receive any of the interest until the bond matures.

WHAT ARE BRADY BONDS?

The U.S. Brady Bond program, introduced in 1989 by former U.S. Secretary of Treasury Nicholas F. Brady, has given many countries a way to improve their credit worthiness. Under this plan, U.S. banks were asked to forgive the debt of developing countries that agreed to privatize their economies. The developing countries who participated in the program were then issued longer-maturity bonds, which in turn lowered their interest rate payment. Brady bonds enabled developing nations, such as Mexico and Brazil, to exchange their existing commercial bank loans for new bonds with more manageable payment terms.

Investments in Brady bonds are collateralized by U.S. Treasury zero-coupon bonds with the same maturity as the Brady bonds, with interest payments collateralized by cash securities equal to one year of rolling interest payments. Boiling that all down into a nutshell, Brady bonds are a method for the U.S. government to help investors feel more secure about investing in bonds of developing nations.

WHAT ARE SOME OF THE FACTORS THAT AFFECT THE RETURNS ON FOREIGN GOVERNMENT BONDS FOR U.S. INVESTORS?

For the most part, the same factors that affect U.S. bonds—interest rate levels, credit market conditions (that is, how willing banks are to lend money), actual and expected inflation, and the rate of economic growth, to name a few. Naturally, a bond's price also reflects its particular characteristics such as credit quality, maturity, and supply/demand situations.

But there are also important differences that can make foreign government bonds riskier. Many countries are less stable politically than the U.S. and have less diverse economies. Political or economic upheaval in such a country could jeopardize local bond markets, so an investor must continually monitor and interpret the internal developments of the countries in which he or she invests. This risk, however, can be greatly reduced by investing in government bonds of developed nations.

SHOULD I WORRY ABOUT THE VALUE OF THE CURRENCY IN WHICH MY OVERSEAS BONDS ARE DENOMINATED?

Yes. Currency translation probably generates the greatest day-to-day concern for the foreign bond investor. Initially, dollars must be converted to the local currency to purchase a local bond. Subsequently, price quotations, interest, and any sale or redemption proceeds must be converted from that foreign currency back into U.S. dollars. Because foreign exchange rates fluctuate constantly, currency movements can increase or decrease the bond's dollar value and investment return even if the bond's price remains unchanged. In my opinion, hiring a professional to select, manage, and constantly supervise a portfolio of foreign government bonds can be an effective way to manage the risks of foreign investing.

HOW ARE FOREIGN BONDS TRADED?

Virtually all foreign bonds trade in electronic, over-the-counter markets, as opposed to more formal and regulated markets like the New York Stock Exchange. Information about the various international markets (many of which are quite sophisticated) is available to international investors every day by high-speed computer and satellite communications. Many of these markets trade 24 hours a day.

SHOULD I INVEST ONLY IN BONDS FROM DEVELOPED COUNTRIES?

Not necessarily. To really consider international bonds as an investment category, it's prudent to break them up into two categories: bonds of developed countries, such as the U.S., Germany, and the Netherlands, and bonds of emerging-market countries, such as Korea, Mexico, and Brazil. You will find that bonds from emerging markets have done quite well at times, and bonds from the developed countries have not always done as well.

Because past performance does not predict future results or even short-term swings in the different sectors of international bonds, the best way to potentially reduce risk is to have both types of bonds in your portfolio. Diversification can help reduce the risk and volatility in the emerging markets. In addition, diversification may reduce the exchange rate risk associated with foreign securities. By spreading your investments over many countries worldwide you would be exposed to a broad range of currencies, which means you do not have to rely on predicting the future of any single currency.

The beauty of some of these emerging-market bond investments is that countries that once were third-world economies are slowly developing; unfortunately, some former superpowers are slowly deteriorating. As always, the emphasis is clearly on research—having a good portfolio manager who can analyze the overall risk of each economy is your best bet.

IF THE DOLLAR IS STRONG, HOW DOES THAT AFFECT THE VALUE OF OVERSEAS BONDS?

One trend that hurt the performance of international bonds in the 1990s is the ever-growing strength of the U.S. dollar versus foreign currencies. A colleague of mine who is a top economist refers to the U.S. dollar as "King Dollar" because everyone on the planet wants to own U.S. dollars. Our currency has been not just leading the pack but climbing for over a decade without hesitation.

Going forward, one of two scenarios could play out: The dollar continues to gain strength against foreign currencies, or it adjusts a little bit as some economies, such as Japan's, continue to pull out of their deep recessions. The global bond investor probably hopes the dollar's value weakens, as this would increase the value of his or her investment. For example, if you own a Spanish government bond yielding 10 percent interest and the U.S. dollar weakens 5 percent versus the Spanish peseta, not only do you collect your 10 percent interest but the value of the Spanish government bond should increase by 5 percent due to currency fluctuation.

DOES IT MAKE SENSE TO INVEST IN INTERNATIONAL BOND FUNDS?

Since more than 60 percent of the world's government bonds are from outside the U.S., global or international bond funds (the difference being that the former invest everywhere in the world, and the latter invest everywhere but the U.S.) offer investors substantial opportunities for diversification. Such diversification reduces the risks associated with global and international investing. The major economies around the world generally do not move up and down at the same time. As the U.S. emerges from a recession, the U.K. may be just entering one, and Germany may still be in the middle of one. While Italy may be trying to stimulate its economy by lowering interest rates, Canada may be raising interest rates in order to curtail inflation. If you invest in different world bond markets, you ensure that you will not be at the mercy of any one country's political environment or fiscal policy.

As with any investment that offers a high current income, global and international funds can be an integral component of a retirement plan. The major risk that an investor faces is the risk of currency fluctuation, such as when the values of the Japanese yen or German mark rise or fall against the value of the U.S. dollar. Most good funds manage this risk by diversifying—that is, making sure that the fund holds government bonds of many industrialized nations around the world. An interesting note: When compared to nine bond markets in industrialized nations from 1984–1994, the U.S. bond market ranked last, with a 10.1 percent average annual U.S. dollar return; Japan's bond market was the top performer, with a 17.8 percent return.

HOW SHOULD I CHOOSE FROM AMONG THE DIFFERENT TYPES OF OVERSEAS BOND FUNDS?

An investor needs to make two major decisions: what type of fund to invest in—a global, international, or world fund—and whether he or she wants to invest for the short or long term. Global funds invest worldwide, including in the U.S., and thus would be exposed to significantly less overall currency risk. International funds usually exclude U.S. investments except in reserve positions (typically under 10 percent of net assets of the fund).

World funds may or may not invest in the U.S. You need to consult the prospectus of particular funds to determine their investment and diversification objectives.

The short- versus long-term decision should reflect your own personal objectives. As with all fixed-income investments, shorter maturities have less interest rate risk, meaning that their prices fluctuate less than the longer-term bonds in response to a given change in overall interest rate levels. Shorter term global bond funds generally have average maturities under three years. If minimizing risk is an important investment objective, you should consider investing in short-term global bond or income funds. If you would be willing to accept more day-to-day fluctuation in exchange for potentially higher returns over time, you might want to consider investing in international bond funds, whose average maturities are usually five years or longer.

IF I'M DECIDING BETWEEN A U.S. GOVERNMENT BOND YIELDING 5.5 PERCENT AND A NON-U.S. GOVERNMENT BOND YIELDING 8 PERCENT (LET'S SAY AN AUSTRALIAN GOVERNMENT BOND), SHOULD I JUST PICK THE HIGHEST INTEREST-BEARING BOND?

On the surface, this seems like a simple decision. An 8 percent interest rate is clearly more attractive than a 5.5 percent interest rate, assuming both government bonds are triple-A-rated securities by Moody's or Standard & Poor's. However, when owning non-U.S. government bonds, you should also be aware of currency risk.

For example, if you and I earned 8 percent on an Australian government bond in one year, on a $US100,000 investment we would earn $US8,000 of interest that year. However, if the U.S. dollar gained strength over the Australian dollar to the tune of 8 percent, the return on our money for that same year would be zero. Why? Because of the stronger U.S. dollar, we earned an additional 8 percent over the Australian dollar; the 8 percent we would earn on the Australian government bond would be wiped out by the strength of the U.S. dollar over Australia's currency.

Currency risk exists, but can be managed somewhat by diversification. International investing involves additional risks such as potential instability and differences in accounting standards.

You should also consider taxes when making your investment decision.

AS A BOND INVESTOR, WHY WOULD I HIRE A PROFESSIONAL TO MANAGE A BOND PORTFOLIO FOR ME WHEN I CAN JUST GO OUT AND SELECT BONDS OF GOOD COMPANIES, COLLECT MY 7½ PERCENT INTEREST, AND KNOW WITH CONFIDENCE THAT WHEN THE BOND MATURES, I'LL GET BACK MY PRINCIPAL?

The main reason you would hire a professional bond manager would be to help you achieve an extra 2–3 percent return beyond the interest rate that you just quoted. Bond investments may sound boring, but it's quite a dynamic industry. When you hire a bond manager, you're getting the lead manager and possibly 12 or 13 different analysts who work together to diversify among high-grade corporate bonds (which are rated BBB or better), U.S. Treasury bonds, mortgage-backed securities (such as Ginnie Maes and Freddie Macs), high-yield corporate bonds (which are rated below BBB), and a few other types of bonds as well.

There are two dynamics that can be managed effectively when you hire someone who knows what they're doing to manage your bond portfolio. The first is making adjustments in the portfolio to take advantage of the changing interest rate environment. One time, a bond portfolio manager I respect felt that because the Federal Reserve Board was raising interest rates, long-term and short-term bonds would outperform intermediate-term bonds. He made some adjustments in the portfolio, and exactly what he expected to happen actually did happen. Some time later, the same manager believed that the Fed was at, or near, the end of its campaign to cool inflationary measures. So, he positioned the portfolio to be more evenly spread across different bond maturities.

The second dynamic, which is very important when investing in bonds, is doing in-depth research from what they call a bottom-up perspective. A portfolio manager's job should be to locate bonds that have the potential to have their ratings upgraded by a major credit agency. If that increased creditworthiness actually comes to fruition, then the bond price would normally climb, allowing you as a shareholder to potentially capture appreciation beyond your interest rate.

SECTION 3

~

FUNDS

7 REASONS TO INVEST IN MUTUAL FUNDS

➤ It takes very little money to get started and continue investing

➤ You can invest using dollar-cost averaging

➤ Funds are professionally managed

➤ Securities are selected using proven methodologies

➤ Securities are monitored to spot buy and sell opportunities, as well as potential problems

➤ Funds help minimize fluctuation of your hard-earned dollars

➤ You can schedule automatic investments, direct from your paycheck or bank account

T here are three important advantages to owning shares in a
mutual fund, whether it's a stock fund, a bond fund, or
something more exotic, such as a hedge fund or a mortgage
fund. The first is diversification. Diversification is a key component of any successful investment plan, and mutual funds provide it because each fund invests in numerous instruments
within its own investment style, giving you exposure to many
companies, numerous industries, and sometimes even multiple
global markets. The result is that your risk is reduced and your
opportunity is increased.

The second advantage is liquidity. Shares in stock funds and
bond funds may be partially or fully redeemed on any business
day, although redemptions in other types of funds usually are
more restricted.

Finally, funds have the advantage of experienced professional
management. Fund managers continually monitor the economy,
the markets, and the individual companies that they invest in,
thus saving you time and worry.

The most common types of funds for individual investors are
stock and bond funds. While both of those are mutual funds,
often times the term mutual fund is used interchangeably with
stock fund. Table 3-1 summarizes the investment strategies for
stock and bond funds.

Table 3-1: Common Strategies for Stock and Bond Funds

Investment Strategy	Stock Funds	Bond Funds
Global	X	X
Growth	X	
Income	X	X
Index	X	
International	X	X
Value	X	

Both stock and bond funds can be domestic, foreign (investing
solely outside the U.S.), or global (investing all over the world
including the U.S.). Stock funds can be growth funds or value

funds, meaning they invest in either growth or value stocks, or index funds, which mimic broad segments of the stock market. Mutual funds can also be income funds, which are designed to produce steady monthly income rather than significant appreciation.

In addition, there are mortgage funds, which invest in, as the name implies, homeowners' mortgages, and hedge funds, which invest in more exotic types of investments.

In this section, we provide definitions for all these funds; however, we focus on strategies for stock and bond funds, because those are the most common investments for individuals.

WHERE CAN I FIND GOOD, GENERAL INFORMATION ON VARIOUS MUTUAL FUNDS?

You can start at your local library. It should have available reports from Morningstar, Value Line, and CDA/Wiesenberger Investment Companies Service. The reports from these services are not simple or straightforward, but they do provide detailed analyses of annual statistical data, important ratios such as price-to-earnings ratios, and risk and return statistics. They also include editorial comments about the management of each fund, although they will not tell you whether or not to invest in a particular fund.

There are many investment newsletters that are written for the individual investor. They often interpret complicated information from the various reports issued by Morningstar and others, and make recommendations for specific investment products. Some newsletters cover a wide variety of investments, while others specialize in a single industry or company. Some examples of investor newsletters are *Fund Alarm* and *Investor's Business Daily*; The Motley Fool also publishes several.

Many business periodicals, such as *The Wall Street Journal*, are important sources of up-to-date mutual fund statistics. These publications can supplement information from other sources and may include information that is not covered by the other publications. In addition, many Internet services, such as Yahoo! and America Online, offer their own fund information, as do finance-specific sites, such as The Wall Street Journal Online (online.wsj.com) and CBS Marketwatch (cbs.marketwatch.com).

CAN I TRUST THE FUND INFORMATION I RECEIVE FROM MUTUAL FUND COMPANIES, OR SHOULD I CONSULT INDEPENDENT SOURCES?

That depends on the kind of information you're interested in receiving. Raw data, such as a fund's share-price history or how many companies it holds, are better obtained from the fund company itself. Not only is the data more comprehensive, but there can be severe penalties from the SEC if erroneous data is given to customers.

Often times, you hear advertisements or see literature claiming a fund is "the highest-ranked performer in its category over the past five years," or something similar. This type of claim is hard to pin down, and fund companies' marketing departments can be very tricky about how they slice and dice the facts so that they're technically accurate but still misleading. To find or verify this kind of information, you're better off consulting independent sources.

WHY SHOULD I INVEST IN STOCK FUNDS RATHER THAN INDIVIDUAL STOCKS?

Investing in individual stocks gives you a sense of affiliation with specific companies. It also provides emotional and financial highs when the value of your stock appreciates, because a single stock can multiply tenfold or even more. However, the flip side is that it provides emotional and financial lows when the value depreciates.

Stock funds do not prompt these feelings, but they do give you the following three things that are even more important:

- **Professional management.** Pooling your money with other investors' money lets you benefit from strategic yet cost-effective management. A good, professional mutual fund manager is constantly monitoring a host of financial indicators and markets, as well as investments inside and outside his funds. In the 1990s, you and I could have thrown darts at a board and, in many cases, picked stocks that would rise, simply because we were in one of the greatest bull markets in American history. When the investment markets are more normal, however, the importance of strategy and vigilance can't be overstated. For this, you may incur a service or management fee. But it is a relatively modest expense when compared to the fees for individual stock transactions with a full-service broker, not to mention the time to research and monitor your investments if you invest on your own.

- **Diversification.** A general stock fund will often consist of between 100 and 120 companies in 10 to 15 industries, giving you some of the diversification that every investor needs to reduce risk in today's market. There are also funds that concentrate on certain industries, such as health care. These funds provide diversification within an industry.

- **Better prices.** An experienced professional portfolio manager purchases shares of a company's stock at a lower cost per unit than if you were to purchase shares of the same company. This is because a manager buys in volume. A manager might purchase 400,000 shares, for example, whereas you might buy 400 shares. Naturally, the manager gets a better price.

HOW CAN I DETERMINE IF A MUTUAL FUND IS GOING TO PERFORM WELL?

The two basic questions I ask are the following:
1. Are the managers who were responsible for a fund's prior performance still with the fund?
2. Does the fund have a good performance record relative to its peers?

You can find this information in a fund's prospectus, which you can obtain by calling the management company or through its Web site. However, I believe that 90 percent of a person's investment returns are determined by his or her asset allocation decisions. So when it comes to selecting mutual funds for your portfolio, your primary concern should be making sure you have the right asset allocation mix.

WHAT IS THE DIFFERENCE BETWEEN A LOAD AND NO-LOAD MUTUAL FUND?

The difference between a load and no-load fund is cost. A load is the commission paid to a brokerage firm or financial planner for selling a particular fund. No-load funds bypass the commission agent and are offered by mutual fund management companies directly to you, the consumer.

As a rule of thumb, if a broker or financial planner recommends a fund and will not charge a fee for purchasing shares in the fund on your behalf, you can assume it is a load fund and the broker is making a commission. Whether a person merits the commission depends on the quality of the advice you receive and the value you place on the convenience of having the transaction handled for you.

There are three types of loads: front-end loads, back-end loads, and 12b-1 fees. A front-end load is a commission that you pay up front, when you purchase a fund's shares, and it is usually 4 or 5 percent of your investment, with the lower figure more likely for bond funds, and the higher figure more likely for stock funds.

A back-end load is a sales commission that you pay when you sell shares in a fund. The commission can be a flat fee, but more often it is a percentage of the redemption value of the shares and can be as much as 5 percent. This percentage decreases, usually by 1 percent, for each year you are invested in the fund, up to five years. For example, if you sell shares after six months, the back-end load will be 5 percent of their value; if you sell shares after three years, the back-end load will be 2 percent. If you hold them the full five years, the back-end load disappears.

Some fund companies claim to have no-load funds, but they often still charge a 12b-1 fee, usually 1 percent each year. This fee usually pays for distribution-related expenses, such as writing checks or the infamous shipping and handling fees.

A second rule of thumb is this: Only a financial advisor who gets all his or her revenues from fees (a fee-only advisor) will provide you with true no-load mutual fund investments.

WHY WOULD SOMEONE PURCHASE A MUTUAL FUND WITH A LOAD WHEN THEY CAN BUY A NO-LOAD MUTUAL FUND?

Financial magazines often advise people to buy no-load funds over load funds, but a study by Dalbar contradicts that wisdom. For slightly more than ten years, Dalbar compared returns earned by investors who bought no-load funds on their own to returns earned by investors who purchased load funds through a financial advisor. The study examined not just the performance of the funds people selected, but the actual returns that people realized depending upon when they bought and how long they held onto their funds.

Contrary to what many pundits suggest, the returns for people who paid a sales commission surpassed the returns of those who didn't. Cumulative returns for stock fund investors working with an advisor averaged more than 15 percent higher than for those who invested on their own. Dalbar found that people who invested on their own were more prone to panic selling, performance chasing, and trying to time the market. Investors who stuck with the "buy and hold strategy," which many advisors recommend, outperformed by a margin of three to one those who had actually traded their own accounts.

HOW CAN I FIND OUT HOW MY MUTUAL FUND IS DOING?

Many companies have Web sites or automated telephone systems that you can access 24 hours a day for information on your account. You can look in the business section of your daily newspaper, or check out one of the many national business magazines that publish quarterly or semi-annual mutual fund performance summaries, such as *Money* and *Fortune*. Some funds send investors a periodic statement that summarizes performance as well. If you're using a broker or financial planner, you should be receiving statements on a quarterly basis that let you know how your investments are doing. Various online services, such as America Online and Yahoo!, have fund information updated daily, but be careful: The information is generally limited, and if you're checking the price of your mutual funds daily, you're not following the precepts of the long-term investor.

WHAT IS NET ASSET VALUE?

Net asset value (NAV) is the current market value of a share in a mutual fund. The net asset value is calculated daily and represents the market value of all securities in a fund's portfolio (based on their share prices at the end of a day), plus interest and dividends earned that day, less the fund's expenses and liabilities, and divided by the number of outstanding shares. The net asset value is the figure you see quoted in the mutual fund section of your newspaper.

WHAT MAKES NAVS FLUCTUATE?

Net asset values fluctuate daily primarily because the prices of the stocks or bonds a fund owns change daily. In addition, fund managers may alter a fund's portfolio as often as daily by buying and selling securities. The stocks and bonds a fund owns on Monday, and upon which its NAV is calculated, may not be the same securities it owns on Tuesday.

Money market mutual funds are the one exception. In most cases, money market mutual fund managers try to keep their share values at or near one dollar, so that people can equate it to cash. This is achieved primarily by investing in high-quality, short-term interest bearing instruments, mostly U.S. Treasury notes and other government bonds.

WHAT IS THE DIFFERENCE BETWEEN THE NAV AND OFFER PRICE OF A MUTUAL FUND?

The net asset value is the market price of a share in a mutual fund, while the offer price is the price you pay to buy a share in a mutual fund. Mutual funds that charge a front-end load have an offer price that exceeds the net asset value. The offer price equals the net asset value if the mutual fund charges annual expenses but not an up-front sales charge, or if the mutual fund has no sales charge (no-load). Keep in mind that many mutual funds charge annual distribution fees (12b-1 fees), or back-end loads, rather than assess up-front sales charges.

DOES IT MAKE SENSE FOR ME TO MAKE AN INVESTMENT IN A MUTUAL FUND AT THE END OF THE YEAR SO THAT I CAN RECEIVE A CAPITAL GAINS DISTRIBUTION?

I can't tell you how many times I answer this question in the fall of every year. Generally, you should not invest your money before a year-end capital gains distribution, especially if it's a large capital gain. The only exception is if you are investing in a mutual fund in a retirement account. Then the tax consequences are irrelevant.

Let's say you invest $20,000 in a growth mutual fund, purchasing 2,000 shares at $10 per share. The day after you invest in it, the mutual fund pays a $2 per share capital gains distribution. You will receive the capital gains distribution of $2 per share, the price of your fund will decline to $8, and you will have to pay taxes on an approximate gain of $4,000.

In short, you have bought into a mutual fund that is required to distribute all its profits that have accumulated during the calendar year among all shareholders by year end. Even though you didn't actually earn any profits because you weren't invested in the mutual fund long enough, at the time the profits were distributed to the shareholders, you owned shares. Hence, the fund company must pay you your portion of the distribution.

If this mutual fund is in an IRA, and you are reinvesting the capital gains, the $4,000 would be reinvested tax-free, and your account would still be worth $20,000. If this mutual fund is not in an IRA, however, the $4,000 is considered a capital gain, which is taxable, and your immediate distribution would be considered a short-term gain, taxable as ordinary income. If we assume a 35 percent tax bracket, your $20,000 investment is now worth $18,600 (multiply $4,000 by 35 percent and subtract the result from $20,000). This is why it is better to wait until after the capital gains distribution is declared to buy into long-term, growth mutual funds. I equate the strategy of trying to get that capital gains distribution to going into a local store with a dollar and asking for four quarters in return. Most people would not be excited about walking out of the store with four quarters on which they now owe taxes.

WHAT ARE THE RECORD DATE AND PAYMENT DATE OF A MUTUAL FUND?

They're bookkeeping dates that the mutual fund company keeps. If you are the shareholder of a mutual fund on its record date, you will receive a distribution, of capital gains or dividends, on the payment date. You can elect to have this distribution reinvested in additional shares, invested in a different fund, or have a check for the distribution amount mailed to you. The time period between the record date and the payment date (which varies, depending on the type of security) is generally used for administrative procedures such as file updating, statement preparation, and check drafting. Of course, the cash portion of the distribution remains active in your account during this period.

WHAT IS THE X-DISTRIBUTION DATE, AND WHY DOES THE NET ASSET VALUE GENERALLY DECREASE ON THIS DATE?

On the x-distribution date, which in many cases is also the record date, the amount of the intended dividend distribution is excluded from a fund's assets for purposes of calculating the NAV. The fund is classified as x-dividend on this date, and the letter x appears after the fund's name in fund listings. The letter e will appear in place of the x if the NAV has been reduced to reflect a capital gains distribution.

BESIDES PROFESSIONAL MANAGEMENT AND CONSTANT SUPERVISION, ARE THERE OTHER SERVICES THAT I WOULD RECEIVE FROM A MUTUAL FUND COMPANY?

As mutual fund assets have grown, mutual fund management organizations have begun to spend more energy servicing their existing customers as opposed to just bringing new customers aboard. The following are some of the services that they provide:

- **Distribution options.** Mutual fund companies usually let you choose how you'd like to handle distributions. For example, you can opt to have your monthly, quarterly, or annual dividend and capital gains distributions reinvested in your fund account, free of charge, to take advantage of compounding. You can elect to have them invested in another fund. You can choose to have the company issue checks and send the distributions to you by mail. Or, you can specify that they make a deposit directly to your checking account.

- **Access to your money.** Unlike some other investments, such as individual bonds (not in a fund) and CDs—not to mention illiquid investments like real estate—you can withdraw money from your account at any time without penalty. In fact, you can opt to set up a systematic withdrawal plan that allows you to receive monthly, quarterly, or semi-annual checks.
- **Annual tax statements.** In an effort to keep up with the times, many fund companies now provide customers with a simple consolidated statement at tax time explaining how much of your investments fell into the long-term and short-term categories.
- **24-hour account information.** For many investors, getting account information is as simple as dialing a toll-free number from their touch tone phone at their convenience. Such services let callers electronically check their account balances, fund prices, and performance. Many companies also have Web sites with this information, although privacy issues can make accessing your information complicated.
- **Affordable investment minimums.** Many mutual fund companies allow you to open an account with as little as $250 and make additional contributions of as little as $50 at a time.

WHAT ARE INDEX FUNDS?

Index funds are mutual funds that try to duplicate the performance of market indices by investing in the same, or a representative sampling of, securities that the indices track. The Standard & Poor's 500, an index of 500 large-company, quality stocks, is probably the most popular benchmark used by index funds. There are other indices used for stocks, bonds, and other securities that share similar characteristics, such as Morgan Stanley's EAFE Index, which is a benchmark for Europe and Asia, or the Russell 2000, which consists of small-cap stocks.

The goal of managers of index funds is to match, not beat, market performance. The index fund approach is based on the belief that no one can successfully predict, invest, and promote performance of individual securities. An index fund appreciates when the overall market or market segment appreciates, and is not dependent on picking winners within that market. Many business school professors believe in the index concept, and a small percentage of advisors use index funds exclusively. This is because they believe that in the long term the majority of professional fund managers do not achieve even average performance on their stock selections. However, there are many examples of equity fund managers who outperform the market.

SHOULD I INVEST IN INDEX FUNDS?

Indexing has elevated the valuations of commonly indexed stocks to a higher level than they should have relative to nonindexed stocks. A large-cap stock that's included in the S&P 500 is likely to be a worse bargain than a similar stock that isn't in that list, simply because there are more dollars chasing after the S&P 500 stocks. I believe that there will be a readjustment where, ironically, indexes and the securities in them will substantially underperform the market.

Those who promote index funds make the case that with their strategy of buying and holding a certain basket of stocks, index funds are good vehicles for long-term growth. However, because index fund managers buy and sell stocks in an effort to mimic a certain benchmark—one of the most common being the S&P 500 index—this investment generally confines you to mediocre results, rarely outperforming the market.

SHOULDN'T I BE CONTENT TO MATCH THE MARKET'S PERFORMANCE WITH AN INDEX FUND?

A prudent investor considers his or her real return—that is, the amount he or she will make after incurring the fund's management fees. These fees, no matter how small they are, *do* reduce the total return to the investor.

All funds pass along costs to their investors. So the issue for investors is whether or not the value a portfolio manager provides is worth the cost. I do not believe that a portfolio manager who merely clones other investment strategies is providing enough value to investors. They would be better off investing in a fund, such as Franklin Templeton's Mutual Series Funds, which has world-class portfolio managers who search for undervalued securities in an effort to anticipate and plan for the reality of good and bad markets.

An index fund almost by definition is only beneficial in good markets. Index funds may seem attractive because of their basic strategy of cloning the market, but wise investors realize that there is more to consider than just running after a bull market.

CAN YOU EXPLAIN THE DIFFERENT MANAGEMENT STYLES OF STOCK FUND MANAGERS?

Fund managers can invest a portfolio using one of two styles: growth or value. Growth fund managers look for companies whose stock earnings per share are expected to grow faster than their competitors. Value fund managers look for stocks that are selling below what they believe the stocks are worth with the idea that other investors will eventually recognize the company's value and bid up the price.

If you own a value fund, you should consider investing in a growth fund as well, to help maximize your returns. There are many years that growth funds perform better than value funds, simply because the companies in the value fund's portfolio were not embraced by the investment community. Then suddenly, the value fund's stocks will be viewed favorably, and the value funds will outperform the growth funds.

WHAT IS THE DIFFERENCE BETWEEN A VALUE FUND AND A GROWTH FUND?

A value fund's holdings are usually companies that are undervalued because they have fallen on hard times, are out of favor with investors, have been hit by bad news, or have uncertain futures. Value fund managers buy these companies because they expect that as other investors discover these undervalued securities, they will bid up the share price. Finding these companies requires investment savvy and careful research of a company's assets and earnings.

In contrast, growth funds usually seek to buy shares of successful companies with above average earnings and strong future prospects for earnings growth. Portfolio holdings are often well-known companies with superior technology or unique products and services. Growth funds tend to increase in value more rapidly than value funds. These funds typically offer no dividends. Because growth funds are more volatile than many other investments, they also require patience and an emotional ability to ride out the ups and downs of the price per share.

DOES IT MAKE SENSE FOR A CONSERVATIVE INVESTOR TO BE IN AN AGGRESSIVE GROWTH FUND?

Assuming you are a long-term investor, I think that it is wise to put a small piece of your portfolio in an aggressive growth investment. The management of good aggressive growth funds uses a disciplined research process to find companies that are best poised for growth. They target companies with the potential to achieve a 20 percent rate of growth in sales, operating profit, and earnings per share. Portfolio management teams also confirm the strength of a company's senior managers, and whether they have a meaningful personal stake in their firm.

Investors who are willing to take the added risks of these aggressive investments have the potential of reaping above-average rewards by owning these companies and participating in their success stories. Aggressive growth funds historically have generated higher returns than any other mutual fund category. However, you will have to stomach significant price fluctuations. In my opinion, investing in aggressive growth funds is only suitable for individuals with long-term goals—goals that extend out at least five to ten years.

AS A CONSERVATIVE INVESTOR, SHOULD I LOOK AT GROWTH FUNDS THAT HAVE HOLDINGS IN SMALL, MEDIUM, OR LARGE COMPANIES?

As a conservative investor, you should try to invest in all three, in order to properly diversify your portfolio. But your concentration should be on the larger companies, which are by and large— but by no means always—more stable than medium or small companies.

IS A SMALL-COMPANY MUTUAL FUND TOO AGGRESSIVE FOR A CONSERVATIVE INVESTOR?

As a long-term investor, you may want to consider placing a small portion of your assets in a small-company mutual fund. Nearly 90 percent of the publicly traded companies in the U.S. are small-capitalization companies, businesses whose outstanding shares have a market value of less than $2 billion.

Small companies employ nearly 60 percent of the country's work force, represent roughly 40 percent of the gross domestic product, and contribute 50 percent of private sector output. Small businesses are responsible for twice the number of significant innovations as large companies, which creates the potential for aggressive growth. However, you need to be able to stomach volatility, as there is extreme short-term fluctuation in this type of investment. In the short term you will find this type of investment to be very aggressive, but over the long term it is my belief that you will be rewarded for your patience.

AN INCOME MUTUAL FUND I HAVE OWNED FOR OVER A YEAR HAS GONE DOWN A FEW CENTS. IS THERE ANY REASON TO HANG ON TO AN INVESTMENT LIKE THIS?

After the stock market crash in 1987, a new income mutual fund was introduced to the marketplace at $5 per share and I began recommending it to clients. Ten years later the price per share was $4.93, and many people were asking me why they should own an investment that has not gone up in ten years. The reason is because most income mutual funds, whether they are stock or bond funds, are designed to produce monthly income.

The key to an income mutual fund is to accumulate as many shares as you can over time, because the income you receive is based directly on how many shares you own. So, if you've reinvested your income and now have many more shares than you used to have, it's been a successful investment.

The price per share in a well-managed income mutual fund may be the same or a little lower than it was when you invested in the fund, but that's not how to measure this investment. Unfortunately, most investors focus on the price per share, which goes up and down from day to day and from month to month. Because investors are most familiar with stocks and how they work, they often expect other investments to behave the same way and so they watch the price per share. The only time the price per share will really come into play in an income mutual fund, however, is when you want to liquidate some or all of your shares.

HOW DO YOU GET MONTHLY INCOME FROM A GROWTH MUTUAL FUND?

Many growth mutual funds today generate zero interest and dividends. Microsoft has been a great success story for investors since it went public in 1986, but it has never paid a dividend to its shareholders. If you own a growth mutual fund that owns Microsoft and other world-class companies in various industries, all not paying dividends, you would have a growth mutual fund that does not generate monthly income.

The way investors can receive monthly income from a growth mutual fund is through systematic withdrawals. Let's say you have $100,000 in a growth mutual fund and each month you want $500 deposited directly into your local checking account. You can arrange to have the mutual fund company, each month, automatically sell the number of shares necessary to generate $500 and make the deposit. The number of shares it sells each month to generate $500 will vary, because the price per share changes.

When deciding how much to withdraw, be sure that you don't take too much juice out of the orange. For example, consider taking a monthly withdrawal of 6 percent of the initial investment of $100,000. If you estimate that a growth mutual fund is likely to average 10 percent per year return, then in my opinion you are not withdrawing too much for two reasons. First, removing 6 percent for your lifestyle expenses means you are extracting less than two-thirds of the juice from the orange. Second, it is likely that the fund's profit distribution that you receive at the end of a year will replenish the amount you withdrew, if not exceed it. The SEC requires mutual funds to distribute the profits that they realize during the course of a calendar year in that same year. For the past fifteen years, the distribution that many well-managed growth mutual fund companies have made at the end of the year has done a great job of replenishing the amount of shares investors sold in order to have income.

HOW CAN A MUTUAL FUND THAT LOST MONEY THIS YEAR STILL GIVE ME A TAXABLE CAPITAL GAINS DISTRIBUTION?

In defense of the mutual fund companies, they're not trying to impose financial pain on investors on purpose; they're following rules that were established many years ago. These rules state that a fund must distribute its capital gains (the difference between the sale price of an asset and the cost) to shareholders by year end. But how it is possible for a fund to have a gain and a loss in the same year? Let's look at a simple example of the dynamics that occur to make this happen.

Let's say that on February 1, 2003, a stock fund portfolio manager buys 50,000 shares of Company A at $8.75 per share. On December 1, 2003, he sells those shares at $13.75 per share. The gain on this trade is $5 per share or $250,000.

Unfortunately, the rest of the stocks in the fund didn't fare very well this year. On December 1, 2003, with the exception of Company A, the share prices of the other companies' stocks are either the same or below their original purchase prices. Therefore, the NAV of the fund is down.

On December 2, 2003, after selling the shares of Company A, the portfolio manager has $687,500 to invest ($13.75 multiplied by 50,000 shares). He decides to invest in some of the stocks he already owns; with their prices below what he originally paid for them, he sees them as undervalued. (Remember, if a fund manager thinks a stock is a good buy at $10 per share and the price drops to $7 per share, he sees it as even a better buy.)

The result? The fund has a capital gain in the same year that it lost value. The manager reinvested the principal and gain from the sale back in the fund, but this does not preclude the fund from having to report the gain as a gain. It also doesn't increase the value of the fund. The manager reinvested in stocks that had a lower price, so the NAV is still low and won't increase until stock prices begin to rise. Hence, you will receive a capital gains distribution even though your fund lost value.

IF I REINVEST THE DIVIDENDS AND INTEREST ON MY MUTUAL FUNDS, DO I STILL HAVE TO PAY TAXES ON THEM?

The dividends and interest you earn on a mutual fund investment are taxable in the year in which they are paid even if you are reinvesting them and not taking them in cash. Sometime after year end you should receive a 1099 showing how much in interest and dividends you earned during the calendar year.

There is an exception to this rule: tax-free municipal bond funds. When you reinvest the interest on tax-free municipal bonds, the interest is tax-exempt on a federal level, and could even be tax-exempt on a state level if you own bonds of your state.

IS THERE ANYTHING I CAN DO TO MINIMIZE THE TAXES ON MY MUTUAL FUNDS THAT ARE DOING WELL?

To help investors deal with this issue, some portfolio managers are offering what is called a "tax-managed investment style." This means that the managers will focus on creating attractive returns while being sensitive to the potential increase in tax liability. It is understood in the investment industry that a reduction in taxes can sufficiently improve shareholder after-tax returns over the long run. Taxes not only reduce your return on investment, they also prevent you from receiving the full benefit of compounding interest.

For example, if you invest $100,000, earning 12 percent annually (with compounding interest) over 15 years, and you have a portfolio that is 80 percent tax-efficient, your return after taxes is 9.6 percent per annum (12 percent x 80 percent). Your

$100,000 would be worth $395,510 after taxes. In a portfolio that is 100 percent tax-efficient, that same $100,000 would earn the full 12 percent (with compounding interest) over the same 15 years, and the investment would grow to $547,356.

It is obvious from this simple example that an investment managed with anything less than 100 percent efficiency will lose a portion of its return to taxes, and the amount that gets compounded is reduced. A tax-efficient growth fund will be managed with a preference for long-term gains that are taxed at a maximum federal rate of 20 percent. Investment decisions should be made primarily to reach your goals. If this can be done in conjunction with lower tax liabilities, it is a bonus. But remember, never let the tax tail wag the investment dog.

I AM DISAPPOINTED WITH THE RECENT PERFORMANCE OF MY MUTUAL FUNDS AND I AM THINKING ABOUT SELLING THEM. WHAT DO YOU THINK?

Investors are often tempted to jump ship when their investments aren't performing to their expectations. Ideally, the decision to sell a mutual fund should be based on your overall financial strategy. Selling your mutual fund may trigger taxes and sales charges, and your asset allocation will certainly be affected. In addition, if you bail out too soon, you may miss out on an opportunity for future growth. The following suggestions may help you stay on course and meet your expectations:

- **Don't try to time the market.** Chances are that you will get in too late and sell too early. According to a University of Michigan study, 95 percent of the market's total gains were realized in just 90 trading days from 1952 to 1993 or 1.2 percent of the days that the market was open to investors.
- **Research first.** Read the prospectuses carefully. Make sure that the funds you are buying match your objectives. If you are uncertain, consult a financial professional. If you are comfortable with a fund from the beginning, you are more likely to stay with it.
- **Invest consistently.** This eliminates the dilemma of when to invest. If you keep investing even when your fund's price per share declines, you will be able to buy more shares.

These suggestions do not guarantee a profit, or protect
against a loss in declining markets, but they are an effective way
to build your holdings.

WHY WOULD I CONSIDER INVESTING IN AN OVERSEAS FUND?

In the past twenty-five years, the percentage of the world's capital represented by foreign securities has risen dramatically.
According to Morgan Stanley Capital, international/foreign stock
accounted for nearly two-thirds of the world's capital by 1995.
That same year, Salomon Brothers reported that more than 50
percent of the world's bonds originated overseas. Companies such
as RCA, Nestlé, and Goodrich Tires are all based outside of the
United States.

As different countries, including the United States, experience different stages of an economic cycle, investing in foreign
companies can provide a great way to diversify your investment
portfolio. Foreign markets have historically outperformed the
broad U.S. stock market. Even so, international funds do involve
special risks—political and economic uncertainties as well as
currency rate fluctuations. Based on their impressive growth
potential, however, it makes sense for long-term investors to consider devoting at least part of their investment portfolio to funds
that hold foreign securities.

WHAT IS THE DIFFERENCE BETWEEN AN INTERNATIONAL FUND AND A GLOBAL FUND?

International funds, also referred to as foreign funds, invest in
securities that are issued outside of the United States. A global
fund is similar, but can invest in companies based in the United
States as well as those based overseas. As a result, global funds
may offer more diversification than international funds.

WHAT KIND OF SECURITIES WOULD YOU FIND IN A GLOBAL FUND?

Typically, the companies in a global fund would be predomi-
nantly based outside of the U.S. Although they may do a lot of

business in the U.S., their home base is elsewhere. Some examples of these global companies are Bayer, Shell Oil, and Philips.

To determine the names of the companies included in a particular fund, review that fund's semi-annual report or prospectus. These publications contain a lot of information about the fund. You can request them by contacting your broker, certified financial planner, or the fund company itself. Sometimes they are available for downloading from the fund company's Web site. If you look a little deeper at the products you buy, whether toothpaste, cereal, cellular phones, or light bulbs, you will find that a good majority of them are produced by non-U.S. companies.

HOW DOES A GLOBAL OR INTERNATIONAL STOCK MUTUAL FUND MANAGE ITS INVESTORS' MONEY?

International and global stock mutual fund managers try to balance country diversification, company selection, and currency fluctuation when making investments. The managers of the funds first assess which regions and countries look attractive, and strive to make sure that investments in any single country are not heavy enough to cause excessive volatility in performance. They adjust the fund's weighted investment by country every three months. They also take into consideration current market prices as well as the current economic and political outlooks for each country.

Next, the portfolio managers actively research and monitor over 3,500 companies worldwide, looking for stocks that are priced below the market and below what the analysts believe to be their actual worth.

The value of a country's currency can change from day to day, providing an opportunity for gains or a potential for losses. So, finally, international portfolio managers use a variety of hedging strategies to help counter the effects of currency fluctuation in an attempt to protect the dollar value of the fund's holdings. Some experienced portfolio managers and analysts are part of a team of over a hundred investment professionals who are located in cities such as Boston, London, and Tokyo, and who stay tuned in to the local economies in which they are investing. Be sure to think about your time frame and financial goals when investing in international or global investments.

DOES IT MAKE SENSE TO ADD AN INTERNATIONAL BOND FUND TO A LONG-TERM INVESTOR'S PORTFOLIO?

Many of the world's bonds are from outside the U.S., so an investor can diversify by investing in international or global bond markets. For example, 60 percent of the world's government bonds are from countries other than the U.S. The nomenclature is the same as for stock funds: International (or foreign) bond funds invest in fixed-income securities outside the U.S.; global (or world) bond funds invest around the world, including the U.S.

Foreign bond funds normally offer higher yields than their U.S. counterparts, but also carry additional risk. Global bonds enjoy higher yields than a pure U.S. bond portfolio and carry additional risk as well, but they afford less risk than a foreign bond fund.

The major world economies do not always expand and contract at the same time. As the U.S. climbs out of a recession, Japan may be just entering one, and Germany may still be in the middle of one. While Italy may be trying to stimulate its economy by lowering interest rates, Canada may be raising interest rates in order to curtail inflation. By investing in different world bond markets, you ensure that you will not be at the mercy of any one country's political environment or fiscal policy.

The major risk that an investor in a foreign or global bond fund faces is the risk of currency fluctuation, such as the value of the Japanese yen versus the U.S. dollar or the German mark. Most good funds manage this risk by making sure that the fund holds bonds of many industrialized nations around the world.

I READ ABOUT THE HEDGE FUNDS THAT HAD TO GET BAILED OUT. HOW DO I KNOW THAT I'M NOT AT RISK LIKE THIS WITH MY FUNDS?

A lot of hedge funds have minimum investments of somewhere between $5 million and $10 million, so I wouldn't worry about getting into one unawares. However, I'll explain how they work. Let's say you want to buy a ten-year, $100 Russian government bond, but because you only have $4, you decide to borrow the rest: $96 at 5 percent interest. Because Russian government bonds have low credit worthiness, they have to pay a high interest rate, say 15 percent, in order to borrow other people's money.

This is good for you, because you are collecting this high interest rate. You'll be able to pay off what you borrowed in eight years and keep the remaining two years' interest.

This is how hedge funds operate; it is called leveraging of one's assets or buying on margin. It is a risky proposition, because if your investments do not return the income you expect, you can quickly become swamped in debt. To illustrate, let's continue with our example.

Suppose now that the value of the $100 Russian government bond declines to $10. They're going to be paying it off in Russian currency, so the value of your interest payments declines by 90 percent as well. You were expecting $15 annually, but you're getting more like $1.50. Unfortunately, you still owe $96 plus interest to the people from whom you borrowed to buy the $100 bond. How are you going to pay them off?

Hedge funds have historically made a lot of money for a lot of wealthy people, but they are risky. What happened in the more widely reported cases was that some intelligent people who created sophisticated computer models made some very bad decisions. In the most famous case, Long Term Capital Management, there were Nobel Prize-winning mathematicians who thought they had found unbreakable trends in the bond market, and the fund borrowed millions to invest in those numbers. When they proved wrong, all of Wall Street had to help bail them out.

WHAT IS A DERIVATIVE?

The term derivative applies to any investment whose value is based on or *derived* from an index, interest rate, exchange rate or security, commodity, or other asset.

Derivatives may be used by mutual fund and other companies to hedge interest rate and currency risks, to substitute for direct investments in underlying instruments, or to enhance returns. Some types of derivatives, such as put and call options and futures, have been in common use for years. Some newer ones, however, have magnified investors' exposure to risk and caused losses. For example, in 1994, a small number of funds (notably some money market and short-term government bond funds that are normally perceived as a group to be low-risk vehicles) experienced losses when they were caught owning derivatives during the acceleration of interest rates. Most people who invested in derivatives at the time did not understand exactly how risky they were as an investment—including Orange County, California, which filed for bankruptcy due to the erosion of capital from their derivative investments.

WHAT IS A CMO?

CMOs, or Collateralized Mortgage Obligations, are innovative investment vehicles that offer regular payments of income, relative safety, and some notable interest rate advantages over other fixed-income investments of comparable credit quality. While CMOs offer advantages to investors, they also carry certain risks.

A CMO begins with a mortgage loan, extended by a financial institution (a commercial bank, or a mortgage company) to finance a borrower's home or other real estate. Over the life of a mortgage loan, the interest part of the payment typically comprises the majority of the payment in the early years and gradually declines as the principal component increases. Mortgage lenders will pool groups of loans with similar characteristics to create securities or sell the loans to issuers of securities. This allows a bank to obtain funds to make more loans. The securities most commonly created from these pools of mortgages are "mortgage pass-through securities," often referred to as mortgage-backed securities. With mortgage-backed securities, homeowners sometimes prepay the mortgage loan by selling the property, refinancing the mortgage, or otherwise just paying off the loan. This prepayment results in the investor receiving principal before anticipated.

CMOs were developed to offer investors a wider range of investment time frames and greater cash flow certainty than had previously been available with mortgage pass-through securities. The CMO is structured to enable the issuer to direct the principal and interest cash flow generated by the collateral of mortgages into different buckets in an organized, prescribed manner. This allows a CMO to be structured to customize the security for different investment objectives. As you can see, it's very similar to a bond, so as traditional bonds behave, as interest rates rise, the price of your CMO would normally decline. On the other hand, as interest rates decline, the prices of your CMO should rise. The challenge is that there is such a wide variety of CMO securities with different cash flow, expected maturity characteristics, and so on. There is a positive and negative to this. The positive is that you can own a CMO that meets your specific investment objectives. The negative is that the many different alternatives can create confusion to the investor.

SECTION 4

~

INVESTING

7 COMMON MISTAKES INVESTORS MAKE

➤ Calculating their rate of return without including inflation, taxes, and fees

➤ Expecting an unrealistically high rate of return

➤ Not having a plan, or having one but not sticking to it

➤ Taking advice from family and friends without doing their own homework

➤ Measuring success over too short a period of time

➤ Thinking only about the upside of an investment, not the downside

➤ Selecting investments based on their track record

T here is more to investing than picking which stocks or
      bonds or mutual funds to buy. Certain strategies make
      sense—or in some cases, should be avoided—no matter
what your investment vehicles or investment goals are. This section discusses the concepts—from risk to asset allocation, from
dollar-cost averaging to market timing—that every investor
should know as he or she goes about building a portfolio.

WHAT IS RISK AS IT RELATES TO INVESTMENTS?

Many investors see risk in terms of the likelihood of losing their
investment principal. This fear is real and important. In many
cases, the fear of losing principal has a direct correlation to their
memories of the Great Depression or memories ingrained by
their parents and grandparents. Professional investment managers who manage money for conservative shareholders see risk
not only in terms of the potential for losing investment principal,
but also in terms of the rate of fluctuation in the value of the
investments. Even if conservative investors aren't at risk for losing their investments, they still do not want to see their stake in
a high-tech stock fund increase by 40 percent one year only to
decline by 30 percent the next.

WHAT ARE THE RISKS FOR INDIVIDUAL INVESTORS?

Some of the most common risks for individual investors are the
following:
* Buying when prices are high and selling when prices are low
* Failing to set goals, or failing to establish a plan to achieve
  their goals
* Having unrealistic expectations for an investment
* Allowing emotions to drive investment decisions
* Failing to diversify assets
* Forgetting to account for inflation, because higher prices will
  rob a nest egg of its future purchasing value
* Confusing fluctuation of market prices with actual loss of
  capital (if the market fluctuates and the prices of your invest-
  ments decline, you haven't lost your capital unless you sell at
  the low price)

You can control or manage your risk by recognizing the common mistakes investors make and avoiding them.

WHAT ARE THE RISKS ASSOCIATED WITH INVESTMENTS THEMSELVES?

For almost every investment, there is market risk, because the prices of securities rise and fall. For stocks, there is company risk; that is, a number of issues could crop up that negatively affect a company's financial status. Economic risks encompass the impact of an economic slowdown and its effects on profits. This would have a negative impact on stocks, yet since an economic slowdown can cause interest rates to decline, values of high-quality bonds tend to go up in an inverse relationship to stocks, in other words complementing stocks. For bonds, a major risk is credit risk, the potential inability of the bond's issuer or its insurer to pay the interest and principal to the bond owner. Affecting both is interest rate risk: the possibility that interest rates will rise, pushing bond prices lower and deflating the value of stocks.

HOW DO RISK AND RETURN INTERACT IN A PORTFOLIO?

In general, the riskier an investment is, the greater its potential return should be. A small company that's just gone public has the possibility of seeing its share price multiply twenty-fold, or go to zero. Coca-Cola, on the other hand, is highly unlikely to do either.

The principle that explains the relationship between risk and return is called "Modern Portfolio Theory." In 1952, a twenty-five-year-old University of Chicago graduate student named Harry M. Markowitz examined investment risk and reward in his doctoral dissertation. He showed that it was not only possible to measure risk as part of an investor's overall return, but that risk might actually be reduced by employing certain investing techniques, mainly diversification. In other words, the riskiness of a certain portfolio could be quantified and controlled just as returns could be.

An important principle of the theory asserts that an investor can reduce the level of risk in a portfolio by including investments that tend to react in opposite ways to the same circumstances. Even high-risk, high-return assets can be combined into a portfolio that becomes less risky than any of its parts.

In 1990, Markowitz won a Nobel Prize in Economic Science for the Modern Portfolio Theory, and today it is regarded as one of the most important analytical tools in finance. It is used widely by money managers in an effort to maximize return for any given level of risk. Ironically, his professors at the University of Chicago did not recognize the significance of his work in 1952 and nearly did not grant him his degree.

HOW DO I DETERMINE MY RISK TOLERANCE?

That's a tricky question, and one that each investor needs to answer on his or her own. Your risk tolerance encompasses not just the amount of money you're willing to lose in order to shoot for higher rewards, but how low a return you'll settle for. There's also volatility to be considered. Can you stomach a 30 percent drop in your stock portfolio? If not, you had better steer clear of tech stocks, or even small-cap stocks. Are you willing to settle for a steady 7 percent return from government bonds in order to have almost no risk of losing your principal? Those are the kinds of questions you need to address, and while there's no simple answer, as you review your investment options one by one, you should discover how much risk you're willing to tolerate.

WHAT IS ASSET ALLOCATION?

Asset allocation is the process of deciding what percentage of your assets to invest in various asset classes, such as large-cap value stocks, large-cap growth stocks, small-cap value stock, small-cap growth stocks, high-yield bonds, U. S. Government bonds, tax-free municipal bonds, real estate, and cash. Once you've decided how much of your portfolio you should put into the various asset classes, you should make few changes in those weightings over the short run, unless your investment objectives change.

Asset allocation attributes its positive results to the fact that the performance of different asset classes usually varies. Some do quite well at the same time that others are declining. Stock prices for example, fell precipitously in October and November of 1987 (down 28 percent), but foreign bonds rose at the very same time (up 16 percent). 1967 was the worst year in the last six decades for government bonds (down 9.21 percent), but strangely enough, was the best year since World War II for small-company stocks (up 83 percent).

Asset allocation strategies take advantage of this lack of correlation to build portfolios that are unlikely to have assets that all do poorly at the same time. Although no one investment strategy can guarantee success, a properly allocated portfolio is more likely to participate in positive investment trends while at the same time reducing volatility when the investment climate changes.

WHAT'S THE DIFFERENCE BETWEEN ASSET ALLOCATION AND DIVERSIFICATION?

They're similar concepts, but asset allocation is more of a macro view of your portfolio than diversification. Asset allocation is an effort to diversify your investments among many different asset classes that behave differently. The purpose is to minimize risk or fluctuation and try to increase the probability of achieving your expected or desired return.

Diversification is an effort to own many different types of securities, without a lot of consideration as to how the various securities behave. Asset allocation describes the asset classes in which you invest your money, while diversification is concerned with making sure your money is properly distributed around the economy so that a decline in any one area won't destroy your investment.

You could have your assets distributed strategically among different classes, but if you hold a high-tech bond fund, a small-cap high-tech stock fund, and several thousand shares of Microsoft and Intel, I would say you aren't properly diversified. On the other hand, if you own stock in twenty companies representing twenty different industries, but they were all mid-cap companies, you might be properly diversified but you haven't done a good job of allocating your assets.

DOES ASSET ALLOCATION REALLY AFFECT MY PORTFOLIO?

Although you may think that the best investment strategy is to
buy low and sell high, studies of some of America's pension funds
have shown that the asset allocation policy is the major determi-
nant of portfolio performance. Up to 93 percent of portfolio performance in pension funds is determined by the asset allocation
policy that pension funds use.

HOW DO I KNOW IF MY INVESTMENT MIX IS CORRECT?

There is no one mix of asset classes that is right for all people in
all circumstances. However, there are good and bad investment
habits.

No matter the size, you should strive to have a balanced portfolio by having investments in multiple asset classes the same
way you try to have a balanced diet by eating foods from various
food groups. And just as you choose foods within each group to
achieve an attractive mix of taste and nutrition, you should
diversify your money within each asset class to ensure a healthy
investment blend.

In addition, you should consider your goals when you are
choosing investments for your portfolio. If you are saving for your
children to go to college in the next few years, choose short-term,
low-risk investments. For the money earmarked for this goal, you
might put 30 percent of it into a money market account, 30 percent of it into U.S. Treasury bonds, 25 percent in a high-quality
bond fund, and 15 percent in large-cap stocks.

If, on the other hand, you are saving for your retirement that
is many years from now, you can select from an entire range of
securities, even those you believe will not perform well for some
time. You might then want to put 30 percent of your portfolio in
small-cap stocks, 25 percent in high-yield bonds, 20 percent in
mid-cap stocks, 15 percent in a high-quality bond fund, and 10
percent in U.S. Treasury bonds. Note that these are examples
only, and your actual asset allocation should be set out (and
reviewed often) under the guidance of a financial professional.

How can diversification help me reduce risk?

Much of the work when diversifying involves properly identifying unnecessary risk and eliminating as much of it as possible. To take one very simple example, consider an investor whose entire portfolio consists of one stock—Chrysler Corporation. This is a risky portfolio, vulnerable from three directions:

- Weakness in the overall stock market
- Poor performance by the auto industry
- Problems unique to Chrysler Corporation

If the investor diversified his portfolio by selling his Chrysler stock and investing in a mutual fund—let's say a reputable growth and income fund that holds stock in Chrysler Corporation along with 150 other issues—much of the risk of owning stock in Chrysler Corporation would be eliminated, leaving overall market performance as the major risk.

If we assume that the fund even roughly tracks the overall market, the reduction in risk is dramatic. Even in the worst twenty-year period for stocks over the last six decades, the market return was plus 84 percent, while Chrysler stock sometimes produced losses even if held for a period of thirty years.

A key finding of academic financial research is that investors get rewarded for taking risks, such as owning a portfolio stock, but do not get rewarded for taking unnecessary risks. Owning only one stock is taking an unnecessary risk since the company and industry risk can easily be eliminated by diversification. Overall market risk cannot be eliminated, and it is this risk, and only this risk, that investors are compensated for.

Sound confusing? Let's try a sports analogy. Playing football can cause injuries. It is a risky sport and professional players are compensated for it. Playing football without a helmet is much riskier. But no team would pay more to a player just because he didn't wear one. The chance of serious head injury is an easily avoidable risk, and a player deserves no extra compensation for taking it. Investors with poorly diversified portfolios are taking an extra risk but are not getting paid for it. They are playing without a helmet.

HOW OFTEN SHOULD I REEVALUATE MY ASSET ALLOCATION?

If you follow a specific asset allocation strategy, it makes good financial sense to review your portfolio at least annually to make sure that your strategy is still on track. You may need to revise your asset allocations because your goals have changed, or because one of your investments has done too well. If your stock portfolio doubles within the year, it could represent 30 percent to 50 percent of your holdings, in which case you should reallocate your assets. The beginning of a new year is an excellent time for you to review and evaluate your allocations.

WILL I GET A BETTER RETURN BY DIVERSIFYING?

You are more likely to see better returns with diversification than without. It seems counterintuitive, however, so let's work through an example.

Let's assume there are two investors, A and B, and they each have $100,000 to invest. Investor A puts all his money in a twenty-five-year security that guarantees 7 percent a year. Over the next twenty-five years, his investment grows to $542,743.

Investor B also commits his money for twenty-five years, but he splits his $100,000 equally among five different equity investments ($20,000 each). One of his investments is lost entirely; there is no value to it at the end of twenty-five years. The second investment earns nothing, or 0 percent for the twenty-five-year period.

The third investment returns only 5 percent a year, for a total of $60,727. The fourth averages 10 percent per year for a total of $216,694. At this point, Investor B is still trailing Investor A by a considerable margin. However, the last investment averages 12 percent a year for a total return of $340,000.

If you add the five investments together you will see that, at the end of twenty-five years, Investor B amasses a total of $644,422, or $101,679 more than Investor A. This is how diversification can work to an investor's benefit.

HOW MUCH MONEY SHOULD I KEEP IN CASH FOR RAINY-DAY EXPENSES?

When you attend the College for Financial Planning to become a Certified Financial Planner, the rule of thumb that is consistently communicated is that approximately three to six months of living expenses is adequate to put aside in a bank or money market account for an emergency fund. So if you need $3,000 per month to support your lifestyle, theoretically anywhere between $9,000 and $18,000 of your money should be held in an emergency fund for some kind of an unplanned expense.

In reality, I have found that people's comfort levels vary when it comes to this. Some people are comfortable with one month of living expenses on the sidelines, while other, ultra-conservative people need twelve months of living expenses to have peace of mind.

IS GOLD A REASONABLE INVESTMENT?

Gold is what I would call an investment of last resort. Gold usually becomes popular, and its value tends to increase, during times of inflation and when there are fears of international instability. Gold can be purchased in gold bars or coins, or more likely through mutual funds consisting of gold stocks. You can think of gold as a hedge against disappointing results among your other investments and give it a modest place among your investments. However, I would not buy gold aggressively. Its value is unpredictable, and for it to be a good investment, you would have to wait for one of its periodic upswings to sell it. I don't think it's wise to place a bet like that.

WOULD COMMODITIES HELP DIVERSIFY MY PORTFOLIO?

Commodities can be excellent hedging devices because they are not affected by the same factors as stocks and bonds and, therefore, often increase in value while other investments plunge. Commodities, such as oil and wheat, tend to prosper when we're experiencing inflation—that is, when the price of goods is rising—or there are fears that the price of goods will rise. This is unlike stocks and bonds, which start to decline during such times.

Generally speaking, commodities also benefit from global growth. If there are more consumers, there is more consumption. As more people have cars, more gas is needed. As more people can afford homes, more materials are needed. As emerging-market countries continue to develop at rapid paces, this could help propel commodities higher for years to come.

Commodities are extremely risky, however. When you invest in commodities, you're betting on what the wholesale price of a product, such as pork bellies or orange juice or cotton, is going to be on a future date. That's not easy to do, because the price depends on many things that are beyond your control, such as weather and tariffs. There's always the possibility of losing your investment if, for example, an orange crop is ruined by frost.

Because of all these different variables and the number of markets in which commodities are sold, management costs for commodity investments are high, too. However, including a part of your assets in a volatile asset class, such as commodities, can help lower risk and provide you with some protection when you need it most.

ARE THERE ANY INVESTMENTS THAT ARE SAFE AND DESIGNED TO BEAT THE BANK?

One such investment is a diversified pool of floating rate loans known as a prime rate trust. In a prime rate trust, the interest rate payment investors receive is pegged to the interest rate that banks are currently offering their best, most trustworthy customers, which is prime plus a couple of points. Every three to six months, banks adjust their interest rates to reflect any changes in the prime rate; when they do this, the interest rate payment to investors is adjusted likewise. You purchase shares of this diversified pool the way you purchase shares in a mutual fund.

A prime rate trust lends money to large companies for short periods of time, typically 30 to 60 days. Some examples of companies that have borrowed from such a trust are Mary Kay Cosmetics, Six Flags Theme Parks, Keebler Corporation, and Long John Silver Restaurants. These companies have seen their credit ratings fall below investment grade, but since these loans are secured by corporate assets, a prime rate trust is considered a safe investment and far less risky than high-yield (or junk) bonds.

In addition, the loans a prime rate trust makes are generally senior loans, meaning that if a company files for bankruptcy, this creditor would be first in line ahead of the bondholders or stockholders. While there is no guarantee that the trust will be able to maintain a stable net asset value, this kind of portfolio historically has maintained very stable prices per share because the interest rate paid to investors will fluctuate and adjust. This causes the net asset value of a prime rate trust to fluctuate less.

An investment in a prime rate trust may outperform a bank investment, such as short-term CDs, by 1½ to 2½ percent per year. It may also help protect against the eroding effect of inflation, because higher inflation rates usually result in higher interest rates. Unlike investments that pay a fixed income, senior floating rate loans generate income that adjusts. If inflation and interest rates rise, so does income. Likewise, if inflation and interest rates fall, so does income.

A prime rate trust is also more liquid than a CD, but less liquid than a money market fund. Investors are generally able to withdraw their money only on a quarterly basis. The investment companies have adopted this policy to protect prime rate trusts against too many liquidations on a single day.

HOW MUCH MORE INCOME CAN A HIGHER-YIELD INVESTMENT PROVIDE AND STILL BE CONSERVATIVE?

When interest rates began to decline in the mid- to late 1980s, many savers started cashing in their CDs for alternative investments, including bonds. The realization back then was that earning a yield that was a mere 2 percent higher could significantly boost your monthly income and help you maintain your lifestyle, and could be done while remaining a conservative investor. The same is true today. A $100,000 investment yielding 5 percent can provide a monthly income of $416. This same $100,000 investment earning 7 percent interest will provide a monthly income of $583, or $167 more.

When people approach me seeking a higher income, I sometimes suggest that they take a percentage of their bond investments as income and reinvest the remainder of the income. For
example, if they have a bond fund that yields 8 percent, I might
suggest they take 5 percent as income and reinvest the other 3
percent, which can provide a cushion from the price fluctuations
that exist with bonds. Each month, as you reinvest a portion of
your income, you will be buying more shares of the investment,
and if the price declines, you'll be buying more shares at a lower
price, which is a good habit to develop.

This generally proves to be a good method of increasing
income, because even though you are withdrawing money, you
continue to accumulate more shares of the investment that's producing the income. Keep in mind that with bond investments, the
yield as well as the value of your principal will fluctuate. This is
unlike CDs, which are insured and generally provide fixed interest rates.

SHOULD I HIRE A MARKET TIMING SERVICE?

The philosophy behind a market timing service is relatively simple: It helps you preserve your capital by selling or moving your
investments before the market drops, and it helps you make
money by getting you back into the market before it rises. Market timers, or tactical asset allocators as they are sometimes
called, analyze the market and predict overall market movement
and the movement of individual stocks. For a fee of up to 2 percent per year, they will use their research to tell you when to purchase or sell investments (usually mutual funds) so that you
make a profit. Theoretically, it sounds great, but the winner is
usually the market timing service. The most successful investment advisors of our time, people such as Warren Buffett, Peter
Lynch, and John Templeton, all disagree with the idea that anyone can time the market.

WHY DOESN'T MARKET TIMING WORK?

Nicholas-Applegate Capital Management of San Diego analyzed
the S&P 500 Stock Index gains from 1983 through 1992, when

there were average annual equity gains of 16.2 percent. It found that investors who had been out of the market on the best 20 days during this time period had an average annual equity gain of only 8.6 percent—nearly half of what they would have realized had they been invested the entire time. It also found that investors who had not been invested on the best 40 days out of the 2,526 trading days between 1983 and 1992 only realized a 3.6 percent average annual gain.

It is apparent from studies such as these that the biggest gains come in sudden bursts. Your primary concern, then, should be making sure you're in the market when they happen. (No one, by the way, not even a market timing service, has been able to predict these bursts with any kind of regularity.) For most small investors whose goals are long term, my best advice is to stay in the market. Otherwise, you may lose through higher costs and lost opportunities and profits.

I HAVE SOME MONEY TO INVEST, BUT I AM NOT SURE OF THE BEST TIME TO INVEST. SHOULD I WAIT FOR THE MARKET TO DROP?

Many people often ask me how to avoid investing at the wrong time. The answer is, invest when you are ready to invest. In today's fast-changing economic and political environments, there's always a reason why someone says to wait to invest. However, a bigger risk is not investing at all.

Let's look at a very popular growth mutual fund (without mentioning any names) from 1969 through 1994. Over this 25-year period, this investment averaged 13.07 percent per year. A $10,000 investment in 1969 grew to $208,893 through 1994. During this same 25-year time frame, we saw terrible political and economic events unfold, experiencing periods of inflation, recession, and political uncertainty. Events such as a president resigning in disgrace (which was also the same year that we had the steepest stock market decline in 40 years), the inflation rate hitting 18 percent (1977), the prime interest rate reaching 20 percent (1980), the stock market crashing (1987), Iraq invading Kuwait (1990), and so on, all could be used as excuses to postpone investing. But the value of this well-managed fund managed to continually climb the wall of worry.

HOW DOES DOLLAR-COST AVERAGING WORK?

As I mentioned in Section 1, "Stocks," dollar-cost averaging is a strategy whereby you invest the same amount of money at regular intervals, such as monthly or quarterly. On the day you are to invest, you buy shares in a security without any consideration of its market price.

Consistently investing the same amount on a set schedule is the secret to the success of dollar-cost averaging. When the price of the security declines, the fixed investment amount buys more shares. When the price of the security rises, the fixed investment amount buys fewer shares. Over the long term, you will discover that the cost of each share you purchased is lower than the average price per share during the investment period.

To see how this works, invest steadily in a particular security for a certain period of time—perhaps a year. At the end of this period, review your records. They should show the price per share you paid each time you made a purchase. Take an average of these prices. The price of any individual share purchase should be below the average. This is because when the price was lower, you bought more shares. Hence, you bought the most shares at the lowest price, and the fewest at the highest price.

I HAVE A LARGE SUM OF MONEY TO INVEST, BUT I'M AFRAID OF INVESTING IT ALL AT ONCE AND HAVING THE MARKET DECLINE. ANY SUGGESTIONS?

The first step I would suggest is moving the money into some kind of short-term bond investments. This could give you a higher yield than a money market fund or a savings account at your bank while giving you full access to the funds. A money market fund will give you a higher yield than, say, a savings account at your bank and also give you full access to the funds. Then, at regular intervals, invest a part of it in one or more mutual funds. Invest the same amount each time, regardless of market conditions.

This strategy can't insulate you from a declining market, but it will limit its impact. Remember that you lose your investment only if you sell your shares at a price below your purchase price. If you resist that urge and ride out a market decline, you will see your investment grow over time. It also should be comforting to know that in a declining market, your entire investment is not subject to the same amount of risk, because it is not in one instrument.

WHY DO PEOPLE INVEST IN FOREIGN COUNTRIES WHEN THE U.S. INVESTMENT MARKETS ARE DOING VERY WELL?

A principal advantage of investing in overseas markets is diversification. A diversified portfolio gives you the opportunity to enhance your overall return while reducing your risk.

Trends in foreign bond and stock markets generally do not correlate with the U.S. markets. While one or more markets may, at any time, be moving in the same direction as its U.S. counterpart, longer term correlations are low. This means that diversifying outside a single market, such as the U.S., should reduce the overall volatility of your investment portfolio over time. In any given year, some foreign stock and bond markets are likely to outperform their U.S. counterparts. Likewise in some years, foreign stocks and bonds as a group will generate higher returns than U.S. stocks and bonds. But neither of these events will happen every year.

The point is that U.S. and foreign markets do not mirror each other often. Therefore, a well-diversified portfolio is a cushion that protects you against potential losses when one market or the other has a down year.

I AM NOT COMFORTABLE PLACING A PORTION OF MY ASSETS IN NON-U.S. INVESTMENTS. WHAT DO YOU THINK ABOUT JUST FOCUSING ON DOMESTIC INVESTMENTS?

Before I answer, let me ask you a question. What do the following products have in common: Aquafresh Toothpaste, Dove Soap, Dannon Yogurt, Lipton Tea, Hires Root Beer, Ragu Spaghetti Sauce, and Alka-Seltzer Antacid?

The answer is, the companies that manufacture these products are headquartered outside the United States. GlaxoSmith-Kline Group (Aquafresh), Unilever (Lipton, Dove, and Ragu), and Cadbury Schweppes (Hires) are based in the United Kingdom.

Danone Group (Dannon Yogurt) is headquartered in France. And
Bayer AG (Alka-Seltzer) is in Germany. Two-thirds of the companies that you and I can invest in are based outside the United
States, so investing in companies outside the United States is an
important part of building any conservative portfolio.

WHAT DOES IT MEAN TO LADDER YOUR INVESTMENTS?

Laddering is a bond strategy in which you buy bonds of various
maturities, so that they all come due at different times. This is a
way to spread out your risk so that a downturn in the bond market won't play havoc with your entire bond portfolio.

WHAT IS A TOP-DOWN INVESTMENT APPROACH?

A top-down approach to investing in stock funds, and specifically,
international or global funds, is when a portfolio manager
decides what countries to invest in, then looks for the best stocks
from those countries. The theory behind a top-down approach is
that country stock market selection can have a bigger impact on
the returns experienced by foreign investors than individual
security selection. In other words, a top-down strategist thinks it
is more important to get the country right than to get the stock
right. If you had invested in Mexico in 1994, for example, you
may not have fared well even if you owned the stock of a great
company. You probably would have fared better owning a mediocre company in another country that had a better year economi-
cally. I am not a fan of the top-down investment approach.

WHAT DO YOU THINK IS IN STORE FOR THE INVESTMENT MARKETS AND THE U.S. ECONOMY?

I believe that if the American investor spends five minutes per
year thinking about the direction of the investment markets,
that is about four and a half minutes too long. But I am an
extreme optimist for long-term investors wanting to maintain
their lifestyles for the next five or ten years. And one very good
sign for the investment markets, which keeps me optimistic, is

that American investors have saved approximately $4 trillion in short-term money market and cash-type instruments. This is money that is, right now, sitting on the sidelines. Once the savers feel more comfortable with investing, and move towards becoming investors, this will become money that will fuel the investment markets.

SECTION 5

~

RETIREMENT PLANNING

7 WAYS TO RETIRE WITHOUT WORRY

- ➤ Contribute the maximum to your retirement plans

- ➤ Put your money to work as hard as you had to work for it

- ➤ Carefully calculate your retirement *income* as well as your retirement costs

- ➤ Don't expect your expenses to be significantly less after retirement

- ➤ Reassess your retirement plan and progress every year

- ➤ Increase your savings as you increase your standard of living and earning power

- ➤ Rebalance your portfolio when necessary

T he number one rule of retirement planning is that it's never too early to begin. If you haven't begun saving yet, it's better late than never, of course. However, the earlier you begin saving for a comfortable retirement, the more likely it is that you'll realize it. Not only do you have more time to put more money away, but investing over a long time period gives you a better chance of riding out market volatility. An added benefit is that the sooner you begin investing, the smaller your annual retirement fund contributions need to be.

Getting the jump on retirement planning also allows you to take full advantage of the effects of compounding interest. For example, if you begin contributing $2,000 per year 25 years before your retirement date, and earn an 8 percent average annual yield, you will have $157,909 by the time you retire. If you delay making contributions until 10 years before you retire, the same $2,000 annual contribution at an 8 percent average rate of return will add up to only $31,291. Even if you decide to make up for the years you didn't invest by investing $5,000 per year (so that at the end of 10 years you've invested the same amount of principal), you'll still only have accumulated $78,227 for retirement.

In this section, I explain common types of retirement investment vehicles including Individual Retirement Accounts (IRAs), 401(k)s, and pensions. (Note that when I use the term IRA, I am referring to a traditional IRA.) I also discuss concepts that form the foundation of a solid retirement plan.

I AM TRYING TO GET MY SON TO PARTICIPATE IN HIS EMPLOYER'S 401(K) PLAN. CAN YOU OFFER ME SOME AMMUNITION TO MOTIVATE HIM?

You might try to convince your son of the benefits of investing in a 401(k) by showing him the effects of compound interest. Let's look at three co-workers, Beth, Mike, and Alan. Each contributes $100 per month into a 401(k) account, and each account hypothetically earns 8 percent per year. Beth started her contributions at age 30 and contributed $100 per month until she retired 35 years later. Mike also started to contribute at age 30 but stopped at age 40. His account continued to grow at our hypothetical interest rate of 8 percent until he retired at age 65. Alan decided to spend his $100 per month in other ways until age 40, and then contributed $100 per month for the next 25 years until he retired.

Obviously, Beth will have accumulated the most money, $230,918, because she contributed consistently over a 35-year period. Mike contributed for a period of 10 years, allowed his account to grow undisturbed over the next 25 years, and was rewarded with a total of $126,129 by age 65. Alan, who delayed his contributions for the first 10 years and contributed $100 per month over the next 25, will only have accrued $95,737 by age 65. Even though Alan contributed for a longer period than Mike—25 years—he ended up with less than Mike, because Mike began saving earlier.

Your son is not alone. Only 25 percent of all those eligible to participate in a 401(k) actually participate. These people are missing out on the retirement deal of a lifetime.

DOES TAX-DEFERRED COMPOUNDING OF INTEREST REALLY MAKE A DIFFERENCE, OR SHOULD I JUST PAY TAXES AS I GO?

I consider compounding the eighth wonder of the world. However, it takes more than one, two, or three years for the effects of tax-deferred compounding to have a major effect on your retirement savings. Over the long term, tax-deferred compounding will significantly enhance your earning power.

Let's assume that between your contribution and your employer's matching contribution, you put $8,000 annually into a taxable investment that has a 9 percent growth rate, and you are in a 28 percent federal income tax bracket. After 15 years, your accumulated account value would be approximately $148,000. If you invested $8,000 per year in a tax-deferred investment, such as a qualified retirement plan, yielding 9 percent, in 15 years your balance would be approximately $256,000. Over a 35-year period, you would accumulate more than twice as much in a tax-deferred account than you would in a taxable investment.

When you retire and withdraw money from this tax-deferred retirement account, you will have to pay taxes. By then it's likely that you will be in a lower income tax bracket, however, and pay less than the 28 percent you pay now.

WHAT PERCENTAGE OF MY INCOME OR EARNINGS SHOULD I SAVE TO ENSURE A COMFORTABLE RETIREMENT?

To accumulate assets and income sufficient to allow you to stop working and have your money work for you instead—that is, retire—you should save between 15 and 20 percent of your earnings. It is very difficult in this day and age to save at this rate, although it would benefit most people to discipline themselves to do so even as they make more money during their working life.

Most folks that I have come across save a certain amount, and as their income grows they increase their standard of living but don't increase the amount they save. The people who are able to save the same percentage of their income as it grows have developed a habit of paying themselves first. This means that first they save, then invest those savings, and then they build their lifestyle around the income that is left over.

Note that I said "invest those savings." Putting your savings to work for you is an important part of the equation. To do this, you have to convert yourself from a saver to an investor.

HOW DO I GO ABOUT PAYING MYSELF FIRST?

Most people I meet fund their lifestyle, pay their taxes, pay their insurance, and whatever is left over is savings. This is a difficult way to build wealth and create financial independence. However, before you reallocate your income, take a look at where your income is going.

Break your income into a four-piece pie chart. For the average American, the standard-of-living piece is 58 cents of every dollar. In other words, 58 percent of a person's income usually goes towards everyday living expenses (food, clothing, shelter, transportation, entertainment, education, medical, donations, and so on). The second piece of the pie is taxes. About 26 percent, or 26 cents of every dollar, is allocated to taxes. The third-largest slice represents shifting risk in one's life to others, otherwise known as insurance. About 12 cents of every dollar, or 12 percent of income, is spent on insurance, including homeowner, auto, health, disability, and life. Finally, the smallest piece of pie is the amount allocated to savings and investments, and is generally around 4 cents of every dollar, or 4 percent of income.

If your pie roughly looks like this one, then my suggestion is to try to reduce the cost of income taxes and insurance. These are the easiest pieces to adjust without changing your lifestyle, which I rarely advise people to do. If you can reduce your income tax liability by 4 to 5 cents on every dollar, and your insurance cost by the same amount, the savings from these categories can be used to increase your savings and investments to 10 to 15 cents on every dollar.

Saving 10 to 15 percent of what you earn throughout your life might not be enough to achieve financial independence, but it's a great start. In addition, as your earning power grows throughout your life, it will become very important, in my opinion, to get your savings rate up to 15 to 20 percent of what you earn—not necessarily crimping your lifestyle, but slowly growing your ability to save. Don't forget, it is equally important to make sure that you put your savings to work just as hard as you have to work for it. This will accelerate your ability to achieve financial independence and retire on time.

HOW IMPORTANT ARE MY SAVINGS AND INVESTMENTS WHEN DESIGNING A PLAN FOR RETIREMENT?

The U.S. Department of Health and Human Services reports that the primary sources of retirement income are personal savings and investments, which, when combined, account for 33 percent of a person's retirement income. Earned income—income people make from working during retirement—is the next most important source at an average of 27 percent, although it's obviously close to 100 percent for some people and zero for many others. That's followed by Social Security at 18 percent, government and pension plans at 10 percent each, and other miscellaneous sources at 2 percent.

A national poll of working individuals taken by the Gallup organization for the Employee Benefit Research Institute found that half of the respondents think they need to set aside $150,000 or less for retirement. That amount may be far too little: $150,000 would last only about 11 years assuming it earned a 6 percent average annual return, and $15,000 was withdrawn each year and adjusted for a 5 percent annual inflation rate.

I'M 41 AND I HAVE $150,000 IN MY RETIREMENT INVESTMENTS. HOW CAN I DETERMINE WHAT IT WOULD TAKE FOR ME TO RETIRE AT 55?

There are two major factors that will determine whether you can retire at age 55. The first is how you invest the $150,000 that you have already saved, and the second is how much you can save and invest over the next 14 years.

Let's assume you currently need an income of $2,800 per month, or $34,000 per year. Assuming prices and taxes rise at a reasonable rate of 3 percent per year, in 14 years, when you're age 55, you will need $51,400 per year to have the same lifestyle. I advise that you plan to have this income come from your interest earnings rather than from your savings principal. This way, you can be assured of having an income for as long as you live.

Working backwards from this objective, at a safe, conservative 6 percent earnings rate, you will need a pot of money totaling $857,000 to produce $51,400 per year. It sounds a little overwhelming, but if you're able to invest your $150,000 of present savings wisely at approximately 10 percent interest per year over the next 14 years, it will grow to $570,000, or two-thirds of the way to your goal.

Then, if you can save an additional $10,000 per year and also grow that at 10 percent per year over the next 14 years, you will have accumulated an additional $280,000. If you adhere to this strategy and remain disciplined as a saver, it is reasonable for you to retire in 14 years.

WHAT SHOULD I KNOW ABOUT MY COMPANY'S RETIREMENT PLAN BEFORE I DECIDE TO STAY INVESTED IN THE PLAN AFTER I RETIRE?

One thing you should know is whether or not you need to remain invested after you retire. More and more companies today are giving employees the option of taking a lump-sum distribution from the company's retirement plan when they terminate their employment with the company. This lump sum can be rolled over and placed in an IRA.

Another thing you should know is the type of plan you have and how it works. Some plans, such as traditional defined benefit plans, earmark your assets with your Social Security number, and then commingle your funds with other employees' assets in that plan. What this means to you is that if the money in the plan grows at a higher percentage rate than your company needs to fulfill your expected retirement benefits, the extra profits go back into the pool of money for other employees.

Some retirement plans also limit your investment options. If you feel confident that, either on your own or with the help of a professional financial advisor, you could earn higher interest on your pension distribution, you should investigate the alternative of transferring your portion of the pension plan into your own IRA.

I HAVE A 401(K) RETIREMENT PLAN WITH MY FORMER EMPLOYER. I WOULD LIKE TO KEEP THE MONEY INVESTED, BUT NOT WITH THAT COMPANY. WHAT SHOULD I DO?

Your best bet is to roll over your retirement plan into a self-directed IRA. Then you'll be responsible for managing and investing your money.

It's important to execute this transaction correctly. One of the benefits of IRAs is that your savings are tax-deferred. If this transaction is mishandled, however, you may have to pay income taxes and a potential additional 10 percent penalty.

To successfully roll over your investment so that your money continues to grow tax-deferred, you need to have your ex-employer initiate the direct rollover. In addition, the direct roll-over check should *not* be made payable to you, but to a trustee or custodian for your benefit. A trustee or custodian can be a bank, brokerage firm, or other investment company. So choose the financial institution for your IRA before calling your employer to arranged the direct rollover.

I AM 60 YEARS OLD AND TWO YEARS FROM RETIREMENT. I HAVE 60 PERCENT OF MY ASSETS IN STOCKS, 30 PERCENT IN BONDS, AND 10 PERCENT IN CASH. IS MY PORTFOLIO TOO AGGRESSIVE FOR MY AGE?

It's difficult to generalize. What's right for one person is not right for another who has different goals or income needs, a higher or lower risk tolerance or tax liability, and so on. However, here are

some questions that you should answer in order to determine
what's right for you:

- Will you need income from your portfolio at retirement?
- Are you trying to earn as much income as possible now so you
  can turn on the income spigot when you retire?
- What is your experience with investing? Have you been managing your portfolio for long enough that you're comfortable
  with how your assets are allocated, or are you still trying to
  figure out a mix with which you're comfortable?
- What is your risk tolerance? That is, how much fluctuation
  can you stand for potential higher returns?

One generalization I can make is that a typical retirement
plan for a 60-year-old should have about eight or ten different
asset classes. Four or five asset classes might be bond-type
investments, and one should be cash or short-term emergency
fund investments.

Another way you can answer your question is in terms of fluctuation. If you feel comfortable and confident that your portfolio
can provide for your retirement even when the market's down,
then your portfolio is probably not too aggressive for your age.

I HAVE A LARGE PORTION OF MY ASSETS IN MY COMPANY'S STOCK. I DON'T WANT TO SELL THE STOCK BECAUSE OF THE CAPITAL GAINS TAX. WHAT SHOULD I DO?

As I discussed in Section 4, "Investing," diversification is crucial
to building a portfolio that will help you achieve your goals, such
as maintaining your lifestyle in retirement. As many Enron
employees have learned, even a high-flying stock can end up
leaving a huge hole in your retirement portfolio if that's all you
own. Therefore, my advice is to sell a large chunk if not all of
your company's stock and take the capital gains hit on the chin.
The financial pain you experience by paying capital gains tax on
highly appreciated assets can be overcome by remembering that
the stock of even great companies can fall. So protect your principal and your gains while you can.

Many people find it hard to sell their company's stock,
because they have positive feelings about the company. To sell
the stock seems disloyal. If this is you, try to distance yourself
from your company, and look at it from a common sense perspec-

tive. Ask yourself this question: "Is it wise to have all my assets in—or my retirement dependent upon—one investment?" Any financial expert would tell you no. If you can keep in mind this fundamental question, it will help you to remember why you should be selling your company stock and diversifying your holdings.

A frequently used financial and estate planning tool for individuals who own a highly appreciated asset—in your case, company stock—is a charitable remainder trust. You might investigate this depending upon your net worth and financial goals. A charitable remainder trust pays an amount or percentage of the trust's value to you or your beneficiaries. If you place your stock in this type of trust, the trust can sell the stock to meet the payments. After your death or a period of time that you specify, the remainder of the trust is donated to a charity of your choice, which is then free from estate or income tax.

WHAT IS THE DIFFERENCE BETWEEN A DEFINED BENEFIT PLAN AND A DEFINED CONTRIBUTION PLAN?

A defined benefit plan provides vested employees with a defined or guaranteed income at retirement for the duration of the plan. An employee's income is usually based on his or her salary and the number of years at the company. The trustee of a defined benefit plan makes all the investment selections and decisions.

A downside to a defined benefit plan is that if you quit or are laid off before you are fully vested in the plan, it is likely that you will receive an abbreviated benefit from it. More and more companies are moving away from this traditional type of plan in favor of defined contribution plans, which give more responsibility to the employee.

A defined contribution plan, such as a 401(k), is so named because it allows an employer or an employee to define the contribution to the employee's retirement benefits, but not the benefit. Employees who participate in a 401(k) plan usually are required to select their own investments from a menu of choices, and therefore, they assume responsibility for managing their own retirement plans, and for the benefit amount available when they retire.

One advantage that a defined contribution plan has over a defined benefit plan is that employees have more freedom to invest their money in what is best for them. In addition, while both types of plans have a vesting schedule, it is generally easier for employees in a defined contribution plan to move their money with them if they should quit or get laid off than it is for employees with a defined benefit plan.

WHO CAN ESTABLISH AN IRA?

Anyone can set up and make contributions to an IRA as long as he or she has earned income or received alimony, and has not reached age 70½ during the tax year for which the contribution is made.

HOW MUCH CAN I CONTRIBUTE TO AN IRA?

You can contribute 100 percent of your annual earned income up to $3,000 if you're under 50 years of age, and up to $3,500 if you're 50 or older. If you are married, and you and your spouse are both working, you can each establish your own separate IRA accounts and contribute up to a combined maximum of $6,000 (if you are both under 50) or $7,000 (if you are both 50 or older), distributed between the two of you any way you like.

CAN MY SPOUSE, WHO DOESN'T WORK, SET UP AN IRA?

Yes, as long as you're filing a joint return and the unemployed spouse is under the age of 70½. The employed spouse can contribute an additional $250, and you can divide the entire $3,250 (or $3,750 if you're both 50 or older) between both IRAs any way you like. However, the contribution to either IRA cannot exceed $3,000 if you're both under 50, or $3,500 if you're both 50 or older.

WHAT DOES AN IRA CONTRIBUTION SAVE ME ON TAXES?

It depends on your tax bracket. If you are in a 31 percent federal tax bracket, a $3,000 contribution will reduce your tax bill by $930. Some states allow full or partial deductibility of IRA contributions. Whether all or part of your IRA contribution is deductible, you pay no current taxes on the income accumulating in your IRA. The power of tax-free compounding is the true benefit of using an IRA in a retirement investing program. Check with your tax advisor whether or not you qualify for a tax-deductible IRA contribution.

HOW ARE IRA WITHDRAWALS TAXED?

When you begin taking withdrawals, the amounts you receive will be subject to tax. If you wait until age 59½ to begin withdrawals, they will be subject to regular income tax. Withdrawals taken before age 59½ also may be subject to a 10 percent early withdrawal penalty. There are exceptions to this rule, however. You may not have to pay the 10 percent penalty if you:

- Have unreimbursed medical expenses that exceed 7.5 percent of your adjusted gross income
- Receive a distribution that does not exceed the cost of your medical insurance
- Are disabled
- Are the beneficiary of a deceased IRA owner
- Are receiving distributions in the form of an annuity
- Receive distributions that do not exceed your qualified higher-education expenses
- Are using the distribution to buy, build, or rebuild a first home
- Receive the distribution due to an IRS levy of the qualified plan

For more information about these exceptions, see Section 72(t) of the tax code in IRS Publication 590, "Individual Retirement Arrangements (IRAs)." You can find this on the Web by using the search facility at www.irs.gov.

CAN YOU EXPLAIN HOW I CAN TAKE A PENALTY-FREE DISTRIBUTION FROM MY IRA IN THE FORM OF AN ANNUITY BEFORE AGE 59½?

Due to the plethora of early retirement programs, it may be useful to familiarize yourself with Internal Revenue Section 72(t). Section 72(t) includes a list of exceptions or circumstances under which the IRS allows individuals to take early distributions from their IRAs without incurring a 10 percent penalty. One of these exceptions is receiving distributions in the form of an annuity. An annuity is a payment of a set amount of money at regular intervals, usually yearly. So, in other words, before you are 59½, you can arrange to receive distributions from your IRA that are equal in amount, payable to you on a regular basis, and not subject to a 10 percent penalty. You do have to pay taxes on the distributions, however.

The IRS provides a formula for calculating the amount of the equal payments you're eligible to receive, and they calculate them using two assumptions: your life expectancy and that you will continue to receive these payments from now until death. Despite this, the tax code only specifies that you must continue to receive the payments for at least five years or until you reach age 59½, whichever is longer. At that point, you can reconsider your distribution options and make changes.

Used in this manner, early distributions can be a valuable tool for middle-aged workers who want or need to take early withdrawals from their retirement savings plans—for example, workers who lose their jobs and are having trouble finding employment may need to tap into their nest eggs for income.

To see how this might work, let's take a look at a mid-level executive, age 50, who is forced to accept an early retirement package. I'll call him Bill. Bill is entitled to a lump-sum distribution of $200,000. He plans to seek other employment, but given his area of expertise, where he lives, and an uncertain economy, he's not sure how long it will take him to find a job. He has some savings, but not a lot. Bill has three choices regarding his distribution. He can

- Take the distribution, pay taxes now (and the 10 percent penalty), and use the difference to subsidize his savings and make some investments; or

- Defer the taxes and invest the entire amount by using a roll-over IRA, and hope he finds a job before he depletes his savings; or
- Roll over the distribution into a traditional IRA and arrange for early distributions under IRS rule 72(t).

Bill's best bet is the last alternative. Based on the IRS' life-expectancy method for calculating early distributions, Bill receives penalty-free annual withdrawal amounts of approximately $18,000 per year. This enables him to supplement his savings, avoid paying taxes on the lump sum, continue to grow his IRA, and avoid the 10 percent tax penalty that the IRS imposes on withdrawals prior to age 59½.

WHAT HAPPENS IF YOUR CONTRIBUTION TO AN *IRA* EXCEEDS THE MAXIMUM ALLOWABLE AMOUNT?

The IRS imposes penalties on excess contributions to IRAs, but you can avoid the penalty by withdrawing the excess amount plus any earnings that have accumulated before you file your year-end tax return. You won't incur a 10 percent early withdrawal penalty either, but you will have to pay regular income tax on the amount.

I CAN'T AFFORD TO START AN *IRA* BECAUSE MY PAYCHECK BARELY STRETCHES FAR ENOUGH. WHAT SHOULD I DO?

Many people feel that they don't earn enough money to spare a $3,000 contribution. What I have found, however, is that systematically investing a small amount of money in an IRA on a monthly basis makes the investment more manageable.

Instead of investing one lump sum, you can arrange to have an investment company take a set amount of money from your checking or savings account at specified intervals and deposit it into your IRA. Many people find that small, monthly contributions are much more doable than one payment of $3,000. If you divide a $3,000 contribution into 12 monthly investments, each investment amounts to $250.

If this is too much, however, invest what you can. Many investment companies require only a $50 minimum investment.

It's much better to start small and now than it is to wait. Investing using a financial institution that can automatically deduct a set amount from your accounts and deposit it into your IRA regularly also helps many people keep their commitment.

WHAT SHOULD I LOOK FOR IN A COMPANY THAT WILL HANDLE MY IRA?

You should look for a company that offers a wide range of professionally managed mutual funds that can suit your investment objectives now and in the future. You want to make sure that the company offers the flexibility to move from fund to fund as your needs or the market conditions change. You also want to seek a company with low fees and annual maintenance charges as a way to minimize costs to your IRA. A few other features to consider are toll-free telephone access and Web access to your current account information, and consolidated statements that list all your IRA investments. These types of services make your life simpler by giving you quick and easy access to your account information.

I HAVE SEVERAL IRAS WITH DIFFERENT INSTITUTIONS. SHOULD I CONSOLIDATE THEM?

Many investment groups or mutual fund groups offer IRA consolidation, which allows you to have one IRA and still allocate your assets among a wide variety of professionally managed mutual funds that meet nearly every investment objective and investment strategy. Plus, you have the flexibility to move from fund to fund as your needs or market conditions change.

Consolidating your IRAs into one account also helps reduce the annual maintenance fees. Your goal should be to maximize returns and minimize risk. After consolidating your IRAs, you will receive one statement, either monthly or quarterly, which will help you keep track of your IRA investments, and avoid the record-keeping headaches that can occur when your IRAs are spread among many financial institutions. Most IRA custodians charge between $10 and $50 annually for maintaining each account.

IF I AM UNHAPPY WITH MY IRA INVESTMENTS, CAN I MOVE THE MONEY INTO DIFFERENT INVESTMENTS?

If you keep your IRA at a brokerage or a mutual fund company, it should be easy to move the money from one type of investment to another. You might want to investigate this option even before you become dissatisfied with your investments, just to make sure you can use it if you want to.

If you want to move your IRA to a different institution, there are two ways to do this. The first way is called an IRA-to-IRA rollover. The safest way to initiate this is to ask to receive your current assets in a check made payable to the institution that will manage your IRA going forward, and then have the check sent directly to that institution. (You could have the check made payable to you, but that could have tax consequences. See Section 6, "Retirement.") Only one IRA-to-IRA rollover is permitted in any twelve-month period.

The second method is called a transfer of IRA assets. To initiate this, ask your current financial institution to send the assets of your IRA to the new institution using a transfer of assets form. I prefer this method as there is no limit on the number of transfers that can be made in any given year. Both of these methods of transferring IRAs are nontaxable events.

I'M LOOKING AT SEVERAL INVESTMENT ALTERNATIVES FOR MY IRA. ANY SUGGESTIONS?

I'm glad to see that you are considering many alternatives. This is important so that you can properly diversify your IRA.

One suggestion is to look at investments that have performed poorly in the past year or two. Studies show that many people believe that the best investments are those that have recently gone up the most. This always intrigues me, because when people shop for clothes or a car, they look for a good value. However, when they shop for investments, they forget to do the same. This is a problem particularly because, in many cases, investments that have incredible performance are overpriced. You should seek choices for your IRA that have the most likelihood of going up in the future.

If you're a long-term investor, and you don't mind being somewhat aggressive with your IRA, another suggestion is to look at small-company funds. Historically, small companies have outperformed large companies, although there is more volatility associated with small companies than large companies. However, should you find a great, small-company fund, don't invest your entire IRA in it. Remember, diversify, diversify, diversify.

SEVERAL YEARS AGO, I STOPPED INVESTING IN MY IRA BECAUSE MY ACCOUNTANT TOLD ME THE MONEY WAS NO LONGER TAX-DEDUCTIBLE. SHOULD I START UP AGAIN?

Whether all or part of your IRA contribution is tax-deductible depends upon your income level, and whether you or your spouse is an active participant in a company retirement plan. I recommend annual IRA contributions whether they're tax-deductible or not. Even if you do not qualify for a deduction, you can benefit from investing in an IRA in the following ways:

* You won't have to pay any taxes on the contributions you made when you begin to see them during retirement. You only have to pay taxes on the tax-deferred earnings that have accumulated as you withdraw the earnings from the IRA.
* Because your dollars grow free from income taxes until you withdraw them, all of your earnings are reinvested tax-free, so more of your money goes to work for you.

I RECENTLY CHANGED JOBS AND MY FRIEND SUGGESTED I SET UP A SELF-DIRECTED IRA. WHAT WOULD THAT DO FOR ME?

The best thing about a self-directed IRA is investment flexibility. When IRAs were first introduced, your IRA could only be invested in the mutual funds that each plan offered. Today, if you hire an independent self-directed IRA trustee (which must be a bank, trust company, or similar institution approved by the IRS) to administer your IRA, you can invest in anything under the sun. The investment options include mutual funds, stocks, bonds, and certificates of deposit all held in one IRA account. The wealth of options in a self-directed IRA allows you to tailor your portfolio to your individual needs.

A self-directed IRA also provides a place to hold investments that may be considered tax inefficient, by which I mean investments that distribute a large amount of dividends, income, or capital gains. Because they are held in your IRA, you avoid current taxation. Your assets grow tax-deferred, which protects them from current taxation, so the power of compounding can work for you. Any type of IRA, whether a traditional IRA, Roth IRA, or even a SEP IRA for self-employed individuals can be self-directed as described above.

YOU DON'T HEAR MUCH ABOUT ROTH IRAS ANY MORE. DO YOU STILL THINK THEY ARE A GOOD THING?

Roth IRAs and Roth conversions are a great retirement planning tool. Any time you can put money into a retirement plan, grow it free from income taxes and, most important, remove both the principal and the interest tax-free, that's something to get excited about. They're sort of the opposite of traditional IRAs, in which you contribute money tax-free but have to pay taxes when you withdraw it.

As an estate planning tool, Roth IRAs allow heirs to avoid income and capital gains tax on an inheritance. A lot of excitement was generated when the Roth legislation was originally passed, but my experience is that for every 10 individuals for whom Roth IRAs made economic sense, only two or three people actually followed through. I attribute this analysis paralysis to physically executing a Roth conversion and the difficulty of exchanging the immediate pain of taxation for long-term gratification.

SHOULD I CONVERT MY TRADITIONAL IRA TO A ROTH IRA?

Anyone seriously considering converting his or her traditional IRA to a Roth IRA should ask themselves a series of questions. First and foremost, is your adjusted gross income or AGI (the bottom line on the first page of your tax return) greater than $100,000? If it is, you are not permitted to convert your IRA to a Roth IRA.

If your AGI is less than $100,000, ask yourself the next question: Do you foresee yourself taking withdrawals from your IRA within the next five years? If the answer is yes, then you should not convert. The Roth IRA allows for early tax-free withdrawals, but only once the plan is five years old, and after that there is still a 10 percent federal penalty on withdrawals before the age of 59½.

Then you need to determine if you have enough money available to pay for the tax due upon conversion. You will have to report the amount converted as income and, therefore, pay taxes on it. According to the tax law, you can't use IRA monies to pay the tax; monies to pay the income tax must come from outside the IRA.

If you do have the money to pay for the tax, have a financial advisor or accountant perform some analyses to determine where your break-even point would be upon conversion. A financial advisor or accountant analyzes the amount of taxes that would be due up-front on the nondeductible Roth IRA contributions against the Roth's tax-free earnings. He or she would then compare that to the traditional IRA contributions and the expected tax liability you would have upon withdrawal in a traditional IRA.

HOW WOULD I KNOW IF I'M LIKELY TO BENEFIT FROM CONVERTING MY TRADITIONAL IRA TO A ROTH IRA?

Here are some guidelines for who would be a prime candidate for conversion:

- Individuals who have non-IRA assets to pay the taxes that will be due on the conversion amount
- Individuals whose tax brackets are lower than the IRA beneficiary's tax bracket
- Individuals with an investment horizon of at least ten years after the conversion
- Individuals with nondeductible contributions in their traditional IRA
- Individuals whose tax bracket will be the same or higher at retirement
- Individuals who do not want to be required to take minimum distributions at 70½

I AM A SCHOOLTEACHER, AND ONE OF MY COLLEAGUES MENTIONED TO ME THAT I COULD SAVE A PORTION OF MY PAYCHECK IN A RETIREMENT PLAN THROUGH WORK. CAN YOU EXPLAIN THIS?

The retirement plan you are referring to is called a 403(b). It is for employees of nonprofit organizations, such as schoolteachers, and you can contribute to it through payroll deductions.

The 403(b) is the only retirement savings plan that lets participants make up for years when they didn't contribute. If you were legally allowed to contribute earlier in your career but didn't, you can make higher contributions using the catch-up provision. There are three options—annuities, custodial mutual fund accounts, and retirement accounts for churches. Each has its own limitations, and rules for churches and church-related organizations are different from those from schools, hospitals, and similar organizations. For more details on how to take advantage of this catch-up provision, see your benefits representative at school, or check out *403(b) Answer Book*, published by Aspen Publishers.

I WORK FOR A NONPROFIT ORGANIZATION AND MY 403(B) IS EARNING VERY LOW INTEREST. WHAT ARE MY ALTERNATIVES?

You have the ability to transfer your assets in your 403(b) retirement plan to another investment firm and still maintain your tax-deferred status. Many (though not all) investment firms that run 401(k) plans will also handle 403(b)s. The process of transferring your investments is called a trustee-to-trustee transfer. The first thing you have to do, once you identify your goals, objectives, and risk tolerance, is to find a trustee that you are comfortable with that allows you the flexibility of investing your money in any kind of investment you see fit.

WHAT IS THE SIMPLE RETIREMENT PLAN?

The Small Business Job Protection Act of 1996 created a type of new, qualified retirement plan for small businesses called SIMPLE, which stands for the Savings Incentive Match Plan for Employees. You can set up a SIMPLE plan either as an IRA for each employee or as a 401(k) plan. Many small businesses avoid setting up retirement plans because of the complexity and expense involved with company-sponsored retirement plans, including the ongoing administration and compliance with IRS regulations. The SIMPLE plan allows the small business to avoid this red tape and, hence, is less costly.

Additionally, a SIMPLE plan allows employees with lower incomes to put away a higher amount of money than they could in a comparable IRA on a tax-deferred basis. Businesses with up to 100 employees that establish a SIMPLE plan are required to match each employee's contributions up to 3 percent of his or her compensation, or to make a blanket contribution to each eligible employee's plan of 2 percent of his or her compensation regardless of whether they contribute. Either way, the maximum combined contribution that can be made by an employee and employer as of 2003 is $8,000 annually of an employee's pretaxed compensation. An employee also can make an additional $1,000 catch-up contribution if he or she is over age 50. While all employees are immediately vested in the plan, there is a 25 percent penalty for withdrawals in the first two years.

Besides the lower costs of administering a SIMPLE plan, an employer does not have to pass any special nondiscrimination tests that regular 401(k) plans must meet, and are not subject to the special IRS rules that preclude plans from having a greater number of highly compensated employees in their ranks. Although SIMPLE plans are designed to be less complicated than previous plans, they can still be somewhat complex.

I OWN A BUSINESS AND I WAS ADVISED TO OPEN UP A PROFIT-SHARING PLAN. WHY WOULD I DO THIS?

This type of retirement plan is a very good way for business owners to attract and retain key employees. Employees participating in this type of plan might stay at a company longer because of the financial pain they would experience if they left before they became fully vested in the plan. However, such a plan is also beneficial from another perspective: Contributing to a retirement plan each year reduces your company's taxable income, since these contributions are tax-deductible.

If you contribute $10,000 to a retirement plan, you reduce your company's taxable income by $10,000. If you own a business in Connecticut, as I do, this reduces your income tax liability by $3,200 annually, and even more in high-tax states. This represents a 32 percent return on your money, through an IRS subsidy, before you have even begun making your investment. And don't forget the power of compounding interest. When profits are reinvested in your company's retirement plan, free from incurring income taxes, more of your retirement money can work for you and your employees.

I OWN A SMALL BUSINESS, AND MY ACCOUNTANT RECOMMENDED THAT I SET UP A SEP PLAN. IS THIS A GOOD IDEA?

Your accountant gave you a great suggestion. A SEP (Simplified Employee Pension) plan combines the benefits of more complicated retirement plans with the simplicity of an IRA. A SEP plan is a cost-effective, convenient way for small business owners to offer themselves and their employees a way to save for retirement.

First, as a small business owner, you are not burdened with expensive administrative and investment responsibilities, and there are no complicated reporting requirements. Each employee is responsible for establishing an IRA that is set up to receive SEP contributions, and choosing his or her own investments.

Second, each year you can choose whether or not you want to contribute to your account as an employer, which allows you to contribute to your employees' accounts based on their years of service with your firm. So if you as a small business owner have a difficult year, you can elect not to contribute for anybody, which would cause you to contribute nothing for yourself as well. There are generous contribution limits as well. In most cases, the contributions can be larger than those allowed for most ordinary IRAs—a maximum on behalf of each employee of either 25 percent of each employees compensation or $40,000, whichever is less. Employees can't make contributions to these plans, but the contributions you make are not considered taxable income for them.

Third, there are tax advantages: You can reduce your company's federal tax liability because your contributions are tax-deductible, and plan participants will enjoy tax-deferred growth of their investment dollars.

Last, there are no enormous start-up fees, and because each employee maintains his or her own IRA to hold the SEP contributions, you will also avoid hefty annual maintenance fees.

FOR WHICH OF MY EMPLOYEES WOULD I NEED TO MAKE A SEP CONTRIBUTION?

Employer contributions under a SEP plan must be made for each employee who is at least 21 years of age, has worked for you during at least three of the immediately preceding five years, and has earned the minimum required amount for the year, which is $4,500 in 2003.

HOW WOULD I KNOW WHETHER TO DO A TRADITIONAL IRA OR A SEP IRA?

If your income as a business owner is more than $15,300 per year after your business expenses but before income taxes, you would be better off opening up a SEP. If your income after expenses is less than $15,300 per year, in my opinion, you are better off just contributing $2,000 to a tax-deductible IRA as a self-employed business owner.

I AM 71 YEARS OLD AND STILL SELF-EMPLOYED. CAN I CONTRIBUTE TO A PENSION PLAN EVEN THOUGH I HAVE TO TAKE MONEY OUT OF MY RETIREMENT PLAN, BECAUSE I AM OVER 70½?

Believe it or not, you can still contribute to a self-employed retirement plan, even though you're required to take a distribution from your retirement account. I think you will find that the immediate gratification of reducing your income taxes, by making your contribution to a SEP, will compensate many times over for the amount of distribution you are required to withdraw from your retirement plan. In fact, I would recommend that you contribute to a self-employed retirement plan as long as you keep earning income as a self-employed individual.

I WILL BE RETIRING AT AGE 62. SHOULD I START TAKING MY SOCIAL SECURITY AT AGE 62 OR WAIT UNTIL AGE 65?

If you are planning to retire at 62, it is generally advantageous to begin receiving Social Security payments as soon as they are available. If you start collecting the payments at 62, you receive 80 percent of the benefits that a person who begins taking them at 65 receives. It takes about 12 years of 100 percent benefits to exceed the sum of 80 percent benefits begun at age 62. The retiree who waits until age 65 to begin receiving Social Security benefits will be about 77 when the total benefits received exceed the benefits paid, had he or she started drawing them from age 62. If you live past 77, you'll begin to collect more than you would have had you waited until 65 to begin drawing your benefits.

I HAVE ABOUT 15 OR 20 YEARS BEFORE RETIREMENT. DO YOU THINK THE SOCIAL SECURITY SYSTEM WILL RETIRE BEFORE I DO?

I think it might semi-retire. The Social Security system is under increasing financial pressure, in part because better health care and longer life spans have resulted in an increasing number of people drawing benefits. As the baby boom generation approaches retirement, even greater demands will be placed on the system.

In 1945, there were 50 active workers to support each person receiving Social Security benefits. By 1985, there were only 3.3 workers supporting each recipient. By 1995, some retirees were already among the first big losers in Social Security benefits. The benefits that they collected fell short of what they paid in Social Security taxes plus the interest those taxes would have earned if the money had been invested in a regular bank savings account. It is projected that by the year 2030 there will be only 2 active workers to support each recipient. The system is going to have to change to remain solvent.

WHAT CAN BE DONE TO SAVE SOCIAL SECURITY?

One solution that I am an advocate of, as long as it is planned and implemented properly, would be to allow individuals who contribute to Social Security to invest part of the money for themselves in investments similar to a 401(k) or IRA. So, for example, individuals might be able to invest two-fifths of their Social Security contributions on their own. In this way, the individual would still have access to some Social Security benefits should their investments fail. However, if invested prudently, individuals would have a bigger nest egg at retirement than if the government invested the money for them. Another idea that I think will come to pass: raising the age at which people are eligible to collect Social Security.

SECTION 6

~

RETIREMENT

7 THINGS TO DO AFTER YOU'VE RETIRED

➢ Continue to accumulate retirement assets income-tax free

➢ Compare your actual income and costs to your projections every year

➢ Live off the income from your assets rather than your assets themselves

➢ Manage your retirement plan and investments as diligently as you did before retirement

➢ Reevaluate your insurance requirements every year

➢ Invest conservatively, but not too conservatively

➢ Enjoy it! You've earned it!

N ow that you're retired, you might think your financial plan will take care of itself. However, just as you had to actively manage your retirement savings and portfolio while you were working, you also have to manage them in retirement. In addition, you have to tackle questions and issues that you haven't had to deal with previously.

One of the first issues retirees usually have to confront is making withdrawals from their retirement accounts. Your instincts may tell you to begin tapping into these accounts as soon as you retire; this is what you have worked so hard for, after all. And most pensions and IRAs allow withdrawals without penalty as early as age 59½ and require it by age 70½. I recommend that you wait until you must take distributions, if possible, and then take only the minimum required. I explain why in this section.

Other questions retirees often have relate to Social Security benefits, Medicare and Medicaid, and tapping other resources for income. I address these here as well. Note that when I use the term IRA in this section, I am referring to a traditional IRA rather than a Roth IRA.

I RETIRED A YEAR AGO, AND NOW I'M NOT SURE THAT I ACCUMULATED ENOUGH ASSETS TO LIVE COMFORTABLY. HOW CAN I BE SURE?

Before you or anyone attempts to answer this question, you should change your perspective. Rather than focusing on the value of your assets, focus on how much income your assets can generate.

One of the most important factors to determine is the amount of income that you need to maintain your lifestyle. Once you've ascertained this, look at your assets and determine if they will generate that income. If they won't, then you should create a plan to build up your assets so they will provide a foundation of income for a comfortable retirement.

Begin with your expected monthly pension and Social Security income. If there is a gap between the income these provide and the income you need, you will have to fill that gap with income from other sources. Now is the time to start thinking about where that income is going to come from. Do you have other retirement plans, such as an IRA, 401(k), or Keogh? Do you have investments in stocks, bonds, or mutual funds? Does the interest or dividends from these or other investments fill the gap? When your assets generate enough income for you to live your lifestyle, then you have enough.

I'VE READ THAT I NEED ABOUT 70 PERCENT OF MY PRERETIREMENT INCOME AT RETIREMENT. IS THAT RIGHT?

There really is no one percentage that is right for everyone. Some people need more income in retirement due to lifestyle changes while others need less. While I would guess that the average person needs about 75 percent of their preretirement income after they retire, I have found there is little correlation between pre- and postretirement income needs.

To get a quick estimate of how much you will need to maintain your current lifestyle, figure out how much you have spent in the past six months. Look at your expenses based on whether they are monthly, periodic, or one-time expenses.

Next, account for inflation and taxes. Most people neglect to consider that prices and taxes will probably rise while their personal income may not. This can force a reduction in lifestyle. What is even more frightening is that by not accounting for inflation and taxes, people run the risk of outliving their assets and income.

As I stated earlier, it's not how much you have in assets now, it's how much income your assets will generate for you once you retire. The upside to all of this is that you, as an investor, control how your assets are working for you. So control them wisely and seek help if you need it.

AREN'T MY LIVING EXPENSES CONSIDERABLY LOWER DURING RETIREMENT?

Don't underestimate the many expenses you may incur during retirement. Sure, you avoid work-related expenses, such as the cost of a daily commute or a professional wardrobe. However, chances are that as a retiree you may want to spend more money on leisure activities, such as travel and dining out. Your medical expenses are likely to increase as well.

In the previous answer, I estimated that the average person needs roughly 75 percent of his or her preretirement income to live comfortably. Using this as a benchmark, if you required $60,000 per year to meet preretirement expenses, you need approximately $45,000 per year to meet your postretirement expenses. Because average life spans are lengthening, you may have to rely on your retirement income for twenty-five years or more. You should have enough capital saved to produce an income sufficient for your needs without depleting the principal.

HOW ARE AN INDIVIDUAL'S SOCIAL SECURITY BENEFITS DETERMINED?

The Social Security Administration (SSA) calculates an individual's benefits using a formula that takes the following into consideration:

- **Earnings.** Everyone who works pays Social Security taxes. The amount you pay depends upon how much you earn, as does the amount you receive in benefits—up to a point. Every year, the SSA determines the maximum earnings that they will credit to individual Social Security accounts. In any year, when an individual has paid Social Security taxes on the maximum earnings, he or she no longer has to continue to pay Social Security taxes.

    In 2002, the SSA's maximum earnings were $84,900. If you earned $50,000 in 2000, you paid Social Security taxes throughout the year and the SSA credited $50,000 to your account. If you earned $100,000 in 2000, you paid Social Security taxes for just over 10 months and then stopped, at which point you had paid enough taxes for a salary of $84,900. The SSA then credited $84,900 to your account.

    When it comes time to figure your Social Security benefit, the SSA takes an accounting of your earnings: your actual earnings if they were under the maximum earnings allowed by the SSA, or the SSA's maximum earnings if not. This is done for every year you worked in your lifetime.

- **Inflation.** The SSA devises multiples to convert previous years' earnings into current dollars, and then applies them. For example, let's say you were born in 1939 and began working in 1955. As a 16-year-old working during the summer and after school, you earned $1,000 for the year. The SSA uses a multiple to convert that into current dollars, and credits your account with a yearly salary for 1955 of $9,230—or what $1,000 in 1955 would be worth now.

- **Best earning years.** The SSA bases your benefit on your highest earnings. It considers all the years you worked, selects the thirty-five years with the highest earnings, and takes an average of those earnings.

The benefits the SSA calculates are those to which an individual is entitled to at his or her full retirement age. To determine your full retirement age, consult the SSA's schedule in Table 6-1. Persons born on January 1 of any year should refer to the previous year.

Table 6-1: Full Retirement Age Schedule

Year of Birth	Full Retirement Age
1937 or earlier	65
1938	65 and 2 months
1939	65 and 4 months
1940	65 and 6 months
1941	65 and 8 months
1942	65 and 10 months
1943 – 1954	66
1955	66 and 2 months
1956	66 and 4 months
1957	66 and 6 months
1958	66 and 8 months
1959	66 and 10 months
1960 or later	67

Source: Social Security Administration

If you take Social Security benefits at age 62 or later, but before you reach your full retirement age, your monthly benefit will be approximately 80 percent of the monthly benefit you would have received had you waited until your full retirement age. This does not mean you will receive less than that to which you are entitled. Rather, your payments are less because they will be made over a longer period of time.

Here's a reference point: An individual who earned the maximum earnings each year for 35 years and began collecting benefits in 2001 when he or she had reached full retirement age received a monthly check for $1,536. This is the largest Social Security check anyone could have received in 2001. An individual who earned the maximum earnings each year for 35 years and began collecting benefits in 2001 when he or she retired at age 62 received $1,229, or 80 percent of $1,536. Today, 44 percent of the average American's retirement income comes from Social Security.

To find out what your Social Security benefits will be, call toll-free 1-800-772-1213 and ask for the number of your local Social Security office. Then call your local office and ask them to send you the form, "How Your Retirement Benefit Is Figured." You must tell them the year in which you were born to receive the proper form. Forms are also available on the Web at www.ssa.gov/pubs/10070.html. Alternatively, you can determine your benefits by using the Social Security Benefit Calculators available on the Web at www.ssa.gov/planners/calculators.htm.

HOW DO I KNOW MY SOCIAL SECURITY BENEFITS ARE ACCURATE?

The SSA sends out a Social Security Statement to everyone who is contributing and eligible for benefits. This statement recaps your earnings record and tells you how much you can expect to receive from Social Security if you become disabled, if you retire early, if you retire at your full retirement age, and so on. It is sent out annually; you should receive it approximately three months before your birthday. You can request a statement by visiting www.ssa.gov on the Web or calling 1-800-772-1213. When you receive your statement, check the earnings record on the statement against your tax returns. If you find a discrepancy, you should report it to the SSA.

WILL MY SOCIAL SECURITY BENEFITS EVER RUN OUT?

No, you will continue to receive your benefits, adjusted for cost of living, for as long as you live. If you apply for benefits at your full retirement age and begin to receive 100 percent of your benefits, you always will receive that amount adjusted for cost of living. If you apply for benefits at age 62 or older but before your full retirement age, and begin to receive 80 percent of your monthly benefit, you always will receive that amount, adjusted for cost of living.

WHAT IS A LUMP-SUM DISTRIBUTION?

A lump-sum distribution is a payment, or series of payments, within a single tax year, of the entire amount in a qualified retirement plan.

MY RETIREMENT PLAN THROUGH WORK REQUIRES A LUMP-SUM DISTRIBUTION. NOW THAT I'M RETIRED, THAT ISN'T A GOOD OPTION FOR ME. DO I HAVE ANY ALTERNATIVES OTHER THAN TAKING THE LUMP SUM AND PAYING ALL THOSE TAXES?

To postpone paying taxes on the money, you have a couple of options: rolling over the lump sum into an IRA or another qualified retirement plan (for example, a 401[k]). If you don't, you'll have to pay taxes on the entire sum.

WHAT DOES IT MEAN TO ROLL OVER MONEY?

A rollover is a transfer of assets from one qualified retirement plan to another. The most common rollovers are from an ex-employer's retirement plan (such as a pension plan or a 401[k] plan) to a new employer's plan, from an employer's retirement plan to an IRA, or from one IRA to another IRA.

For employees looking to roll over their assets into an IRA, a mutual fund company is one of the most popular investment choices, because it gives employees or their financial advisors flexibility in managing their investments. They can choose from a wide variety of funds when investing their money.

I LEFT MY COMPANY RECENTLY, AND STILL HAVE A 401(K) RETIREMENT PLAN WITH THEM. I DON'T NEED THE INCOME RIGHT AWAY. WHAT IS THE BEST WAY TO KEEP THE MONEY INVESTED?

Depending on the type of retirement plan you have, you may be able to keep your money invested in the company's plan. I do not normally recommend this, however, because usually you have fewer investment options to choose from than you do if your retirement plan is at a money management firm.

An alternative that makes sense is a direct, sponsor-to-sponsor rollover into an IRA. To initiate this, you will need to request a direct rollover form from your ex-employer. To complete this form, you must specify to whom the check should be made payable. There's a 20 percent federal withholding or income tax on lump-sum distributions, so the safest way to roll over funds is to have the check made payable to a trustee or custodian, and not to you. The trustee or custodian can be a bank, brokerage firm, or other investment company you've chosen to manage your IRA. If you have the check made payable to you, you could put yourself in a tax bind (see the next question).

Once the institution has received the check, you'll have to specify how it's to be handled. If you have an existing IRA, you could add the funds to that account. Or, you could set up a new account that is specifically a rollover IRA account.

Transferring your assets to a separate, rollover IRA, rather than commingling the funds with an existing IRA, may make record keeping easier if your existing IRA has after-tax contributions. If you mix pretax contributions with after-tax contributions, you have to keep track of each and their earnings, so that when you begin to make withdrawals, you're not paying taxes twice on any money.

It also may prove easier to have separate accounts if, down the road, you decide to roll your rollover IRA into an employer's 401(k) plan. According to the pension regulations adopted in 2001, the administrator of a 401(k) plan must accept the monies (and the interest earned) that came from your previous 401(k) plan. However, he or she does not have to accept monies that were already in your IRA, or contributions made since. In addition, he or she won't allow after-tax contributions from the IRA to be transferred to the 401(k). Therefore, it might be easier to keep the funds separate from the start, rather than trying to separate them out at a later time.

IF I ROLL OVER MY MONEY INTO AN IRA, WHEN DO I PAY TAXES ON IT?

You will pay taxes on the money only when you withdraw it, provided that you make a direct, sponsor-to-sponsor transfer. If you have your employer or another institution make the check payable to you, then the following will occur: The institution making the payout will withhold 20 percent and issue a check for the remainder. Then, you have 60 days to deposit that check *plus* a check to cover the amount that was withheld into an IRA account. If the payout is made in a series of distributions, the 60-day period does not begin until the last distribution has been made.

When you prepare your taxes for the year, you will show that you deposited the check issued by the institution into an IRA account along with a check to cover the 20 percent withholding. You are then entitled to receive the 20 percent that was withheld as a refund. If you didn't deposit the money within 60 days, however, you will have to pay income taxes on the entire amount, and pay a penalty if you are younger than 59½.

Let's look at an example. Jim has a 401(k) worth $250,000 and he wants to roll it into an IRA. He tells his employer to make the check payable to him. His employer withholds 20 percent, or $50,000, and issues him a check for $200,000. Within 60 days Jim must deposit the check for $200,000 plus another check for $50,000 into an IRA account to avoid income taxes. While Jim will receive the $50,000 back as refund, that could be many months from now. This is why many people opt for the safety of a direct, sponsor-to-sponsor transfer.

A SMALL PORTION OF MY 401(K) IS IN THE COMPANY STOCK. CAN I INCLUDE THE STOCK IN A SPONSOR-TO-SPONSOR IRA ROLLOVER, OR DO I HAVE TO SELL THE STOCK FIRST?

In most cases you can roll over your stock from a 401(k) to your IRA, and either keep the stock in your IRA or sell it and diversify it into other investments.

CAN I ROLL OVER PART OF MY 401(K) PLAN INTO AN IRA?

Most 401(k) plans will allow a partial rollover of your 401(k) into an IRA, although I have seen plans that only allow you to roll over all or none of your 401(k) into an IRA.

I HAVE ACCUMULATED A LOT OF MONEY IN MY LUMP-SUM RETIREMENT PLAN FROM A LIFETIME OF WORKING. I AM CONSIDERING TAKING A LUMP-SUM DISTRIBUTION, PAYING OFF MY MORTGAGE, AND KEEPING THE REST FOR RETIREMENT. IS THIS A GOOD IDEA?

As more and more companies allow retirees to take a lump sum of money from their retirement plans, people who might have had fairly modest incomes during their working years may have to decide what to do with what appears to be a windfall. In many instances, a lump-sum distribution can amount to several hundreds of thousands of dollars or more.

Although it might make sense to use a portion of a lump-sum payment to eliminate large outstanding debts, such as a mortgage, you could also jeopardize a secure retirement if this money is not used wisely. Consider that to use it to pay off your mortgage, you'll have to pay income taxes on the entire sum now. In addition, if you are under age 59½, you could incur a penalty. Most retirement plans penalize anyone who withdraws money before the age of 59½.

I encourage you to look into an IRA rollover. The money in a retirement plan can look like a lot, but as people retire earlier and live longer, estimates on how much they will need for a comfortable retirement have to be increased. Your retirement nest egg may have to be a source of income for twenty or thirty years or more. If you roll over this money, it can keep growing as a tax-deferred investment until withdrawals begin.

In most cases, you will not be forced to take a lump-sum distribution immediately upon retirement, which gives you time to make careful, well-thought-out decisions. It has taken you a lifetime to accumulate this money. Take some time to think about the best way to make it work for you in the years to come.

WHEN I ROLL OVER MY RETIREMENT PLAN INTO MY IRA, WHY DO I NEED A TRUSTEE?

Simply put, you need a trustee for your IRA because IRS regulations say you do. The reason is because the money in a retirement account has never been taxed. Someday, you or your heirs will pay taxes on that money. One of the obligations of a trustee is to notify the IRS when you remove any money from your retirement plan. Otherwise, we'd be working on the honor system as to when—or if—we pay taxes on our retirement money.

WHAT DOES THE TRUSTEE DO FOR ME?

Besides what I just mentioned, most trustees
- Produce a monthly, consolidated statement of the investment holdings in your IRA
- Assume responsibility for withholding income taxes once you begin withdrawing money from your retirement account
- Complete the necessary paperwork when you make withdrawals from your retirement account that are either in the form of a monthly income check or a lump-sum payment
- Calculate how much of your retirement account must be distributed after you reach age 70½

What IRA trustees do not do is give advice on how to invest your money or when to make changes in your account. They only execute orders from you or the financial advisor with whom you are working.

IS MY IRA INSURED?

A typical, competitive trustee in today's world will hold up to
$100 million worth of insurance against such things as fraud or
misrepresentation. You should ask your trustee how much insurance it has, and whether the amount covers each individual or is
for its entire holdings. Remember, though, this insurance does
not insure you against market fluctuation or the loss of money
due to bad investments.

I HAVE A PENSION PLAN AND HAVE DECIDED TO TAKE A LUMP-SUM DISTRIBUTION. SHOULD I CONSIDER INCOME AVERAGING?

Generally, to qualify for income averaging, you must participate
in a retirement plan for five or more taxable years. Then, when
you take your lump-sum distribution, it is taxed as if it were your
only income over a specified period of time (depending on
whether you use five-year or ten-year averaging). Knowing
whether to use income averaging can be confusing and may or
may not be advisable, but it definitely is worth exploring with
your accountant.

I AM PREPARING TO ACCEPT MY EMPLOYER'S EARLY RETIREMENT OFFER. WHAT ARE THE THINGS I SHOULD CONSIDER?

Above all, keep in mind that an early retirement means your savings and investments must last longer, and that you run a
greater risk of outliving your capital. If you haven't already done
so, you should review your retirement plan before you retire to
make sure you've minimized this risk.

In addition, remember that you must be at least age 62 to
receive Social Security benefits unless you are or become disabled. If you apply for Social Security before your full retirement
age, you will receive approximately 80 percent of the monthly
payments you would have received at full retirement age. This
will not result in your getting less than that to which you're entitled. Rather, it's a way to spread the amount over a longer period
of time.

Finally, consider your health insurance. Many employers no longer offer health insurance to retirees, and you may not qualify for Medicare benefits until age 65. You should make sure that if the early retirement offer does not include health coverage, that you are able to obtain health insurance on your own to bridge the gap until you reach age 65, and that you have included the cost in your budget.

IF I TAKE ADVANTAGE OF AN EARLY RETIREMENT PACKAGE, HOW SHOULD I TAKE THE INCOME?

People who take early retirement can need income from their retirement plans before the age of 59½, because they are taking an early retirement, starting their own business, or sustaining themselves while between jobs.

If you need to generate income from your retirement plan right away, and you're no longer working, you can roll over your plan into a traditional IRA and elect to receive regular payments. Under Internal Revenue Code Section 72(t) your payments will not be subjected to a 10 percent early withdrawal penalty as long as you take your money out in a series of equal payments. The minimum distribution is based on life expectancy tables, and there are several methods of calculating this level of payment to meet a variety of needs. Penalties will only apply if you change the amount or discontinue the payment plan before the end of five years or before you turn age 59½, whichever is longer.

I'M 60 AND RETIRED. I WANTED TO BEGIN TAKING DISTRIBUTIONS FROM MY IRA, BUT MY PLANNER HAS ADVISED THAT I TAKE INCOME FROM MY SAVINGS AND INVESTMENTS FIRST. DO YOU AGREE?

Yes, I recommend that you procrastinate taking withdrawals from your IRA or other retirement plans as long as possible. Taking money from your retirement plans may be emotionally satisfying, but the withdrawals come at a price: income taxes. In addition, living from your portfolio and whatever other savings you've built up lets the money in your retirement accounts continue to grow tax-free. For this reason, even when investors must begin taking withdrawals (age 70½), I often recommend that they take the minimum required if possible. Of course, if you need to tap these accounts, don't be afraid to do so. That's why you have them.

WHEN DO I HAVE TO BEGIN WITHDRAWING MONEY FROM MY RETIREMENT ACCOUNTS?

The date you have to begin withdrawals is the first day of April after you turn 70½. For example, if you turn 70 on January 15, 2004, you will be 70½ on July 15, 2004, and must begin withdrawals April 1, 2005. If you turn 70 on November 15, 2004, you will be 70½ on May 15, 2005. Therefore, you would have to begin withdrawals by April 1, 2006.

HOW SHOULD I INVEST MY MONEY DURING MY RETIREMENT?

Conservatively. I would recommend a plan that provides safety through diversification. Meet with a professional advisor or investigate some securities that have the potential to build upon income that grows with rising prices. At a 4 percent annual inflation rate, $100 today would purchase just $67 worth of items in ten years. You should try to protect your investment from the ravages of inflation.

I'M ALMOST 60 YEARS OLD, RETIRED, AND LIVING ON SOME OF THE INCOME FROM MY SIZEABLE PORTFOLIO. WHAT PERCENTAGE OF MY NEST EGG BELONGS IN EQUITIES VERSUS BONDS?

Although the ratio of equities to bonds is talked about quite often, thinking in these terms oversimplifies the issues, of which there are many. Here are five for you to consider:

* **Do the investments in your portfolio complement each other?** What I mean by this is, do you own different securities that behave differently in different economic scenarios? For example, you should own certain investments that perform better when interest rates rise and other investments that perform better when interest rates decline. Another likely scenario would be owning certain investments in your

portfolio that perform better as the economy grows and other investments that tend to perform better when the economy slows down.

- **Are you diversified within the equities and bond asset classes?** Not all equities are created equal, and neither are all bonds. History has shown us, for example, that when the economy slows, certain bond investments do very well while others don't. So more important than the ratio of equities to bonds are the types of each that you own. There are many types from which to choose. Investigate and diversify.
- **How much risk do you need to assume to accomplish your objectives?** Often, investors put their retirement at risk, because they focus on getting the maximum return and don't take the time to figure out how much they need. If investments with conservative to moderate risk provide the income you need, there's no need to be in aggressive funds.
- **How much risk are you willing to assume?** This is an important question to consider. Many people, particularly as they get close to retirement, decide to alter their retirement goals rather than make high-risk investments.
- **How risky are your investments?** Many people generalize and assume that equities are more risky than bonds. However, this is not always the case—high-yield corporate bonds or international bonds can have more risk than blue-chip American stocks, such as Coca-Cola or GM. You should review your investments in light of current market conditions.

As you can see, it's not as simple as stocks versus bonds.

HOW MUCH INCOME CAN I WITHDRAW FROM MY RETIREMENT ACCOUNT EACH YEAR AND BE ASSURED THAT IT STILL GETS SOME REASONABLE GROWTH?

A good rule of thumb is to take out 4 percent per year. Assume that you have a $200,000 investment portfolio. In addition, assume you feel confident that you can achieve a return on the portfolio of about 7 or 8 percent per year over a significant period of time. Withdrawing 4 percent of your $200,000 portfolio translates into $8,000 per year or $666.67 per month. It also leaves approximately 3 to 4 percent of the earnings to plow back into the portfolio. This will help you achieve some reasonable growth.

The beauty of this method is that it can give you an income stream that grows over time. If executed properly, as you continue to withdraw 4 percent as income, it will be 4 percent of a larger amount of money. This can help you maintain and protect your lifestyle from the ravages of taxes and inflation.

WHAT IS MEDICARE?

Medicare is a government health insurance program for people age 65 and older as well as people with disabilities. It is divided into two parts: Hospital Insurance Benefits for the Aged and Disabled (Part A), and Supplementary Medical Insurance Benefits for the Aged and Disabled (Part B).

WHAT DOES MEDICARE PART A COVER?

Part A, Hospital Insurance Benefits for the Aged and Disabled, is financed largely through Social Security taxes and helps pay for inpatient hospital care. Its coverage is best understood in terms of the following time frames:

- **Hospital stays of 60 days or less:** After you pay a deductible, all expenses for hospital stays of 60 days or less are paid in full.
- **Hospital stays of 61 days or more but less than 91 days:** You pay a co-payment each day until your 91st day in a hospital. Medicare pays the rest.
- **Hospital stays 91 days or after:** You pay an increased co-payment per day and begin to use a lifetime reserve of 60 days. If your first hospitalization requires a stay of 150 days or longer, for example, you will use up your lifetime reserve and are responsible for all costs after that time. For any subsequent hospital stays, you would be covered for only the first 90 days.

With the exception of the lifetime reserve, these benefits apply to each hospital stay. A hospital stay begins with the first day you are hospitalized and ends when you have been out of a hospital for 60 consecutive days.

Part A also helps pay for a skilled-nursing facility, at-home care, and hospice care.

WHAT DOES MEDICARE PART B COVER?

Part B, Supplementary Medical Insurance Benefits for the Aged and Disabled, is voluntary. That is, you are entitled to this coverage if you pay the monthly premium. This insurance pays for doctors' fees, outpatient hospital services, outpatient therapy, and rehabilitation services and supplies.

Part B bases its payments for covered services on approved charges. That is, Medicare negotiates a price for each service of each health-care provider. When Medicare and the provider agree on a fee for a particular service, that is considered an approved charge.

Once you meet the annual deductible, the plan pays 80 percent of the approved charges and you pay 20 percent. However, if there is a difference between the actual charge and Medicare's approved charge, you pay that cost.

For example, let's say you have to have outpatient therapy after an operation. This is a covered service and Medicare has negotiated a fee of $50 per visit with the provider of this service. If you have not met your deductible, you must pay the $50 per visit. After you have met the deductible, you will pay 20 percent or $10, and Medicare will pay 80 percent or $40.

However, suppose that the provider of this service won't negotiate his fees with Medicare and the cost of a visit is $80. Because this health-care provider is convenient to you, you decide to see him or her anyway. In this case, Medicare will pay 80 percent of their approved fee for this service, or $40, and you are responsible for the remainder, which is $40.

WHO IS ELIGIBLE FOR MEDICARE?

Medicare is automatically available to everyone who is a U.S. citizen, age 65 or older, and eligible for Social Security, Widow's, or Railroad Retirement benefits. It is also available to everyone who is younger than 65 but disabled, and who has been receiving Social Security, Widow's, or Railroad Disability Income for at least 24 months. U.S. citizens who are 65 or older but who do not meet these requirements (people who have come to the U.S. and received citizenship but never worked in the U.S., for example), as well as permanent legal aliens (those who have resided in the U.S. continuously for five or more years), are also eligible, but they must pay for coverage.

WHAT DOES MEDICARE COST?

Medicare Part A is free for everyone who is automatically eligible. For U.S. citizens and permanent legal aliens who are not eligible, there is a monthly premium.

Medicare Part B charges everyone who enrolls a monthly premium ($54 in 2002). While enrollment is optional, as with private insurance, waiting to enroll until you are older (and presumably in worse health) will cost you. Individuals who do not enroll in Medicare Part B when they become eligible at age 65 must pay a 10 percent premium penalty for each year that they delay their enrollment.

The only circumstance under which you needn't worry about enrolling is if you're covered by your own insurance and plan to continue that coverage throughout your retirement.

WHAT SHOULD I DO IF MEDICARE DOES NOT PAY FOR MY MEDICAL EXPENSES?

First, never assume that Medicare will not cover an expense, even if a Medicare representative or a health-care service provider states that Medicare does not cover the service rendered. Rather, submit a claim direct to Medicare and make sure that Medicare processes the claim.

If Medicare denies the claim, consider requesting a claims review. Particularly if the treatment was necessary, something you need to repeat, or not expressly excluded from coverage, you should always seek a claims review.

To ask for a review, send a copy of the Medicare denial back to Medicare with a signed note asking for a review. Medicare patients who appeal their claim denials receive payments about 50 percent of the time.

WHAT'S THE MOST COSTLY FINANCIAL MISTAKE YOU SEE RETIREES MAKE?

Unfortunately, I see retirees making many costly mistakes. The mistake I consider most costly is not having their income from their investments grow over time. People spend a lifetime building businesses or careers, rising through the pay scale, and growing their incomes during the course of their career. In other words, I meet very few people who are earning less today than they did ten or fifteen years ago.

As we build our incomes over time, we typically build our savings with it. The inherent problem is that people don't have the same philosophy with managing their money as they do with managing to grow their earnings. In other words, many people have their money earning income, but the income from their money doesn't grow over time to keep pace with rising prices and taxes. The reason why I believe this is such a costly mistake, and actually the most costly financial mistake, is because it puts an individual or couple at risk for potentially outliving their assets and income, which is something no one wants to do. With people retiring and staying retired for longer periods of time, hopefully more and more people like you will address this challenge.

SECTION 7

~

ESTATE PLANNING

7 EFFECTIVE ESTATE PLANNING TOOLS

➢ Durable power of attorney for finances

➢ Health-care proxy

➢ Living will

➢ Revocable and irrevocable trusts

➢ 529 college savings plan

➢ Charitable lead and charitable remainder trusts

➢ Life insurance

I n this section, we discuss some of the many different ways you can structure your estate to ensure that your assets are passed along, in the amount and manner you want, to your beneficiaries. Two of the more popular estate planning tools are revocable living trusts, which can help you avoid costly and lengthy probate proceedings, and credit shelter trusts, which can help limit your exposure to estate taxes.

Many people think that trusts are just for wealthy people, and until recently, legal expenses, high management costs, and substantial investment minimums have kept large numbers of investors from establishing trusts. The trust structures we discuss here are simplified, allowing many more people to take advantage of them and make use of their estate planning features.

There are several other ways to limit or avoid estate taxes as well: The Unlimited Marital Deduction lets you pass along your estate to your spouse tax-free, no matter its value; the Unified Gift and Estate Tax Credit lets you give gifts of up to $11,000 per person per year and a certain lifetime amount of assets to anyone tax-free; and investing in 529 college savings plans makes it easy to pass on assets to children tax-free for educational purposes.

As with most financial planning issues, if you haven't already begun, the time to get started planning your estate is now.

WHAT IS A TRUST?

A trust is a legal arrangement under which you (the trustor) transfer fiduciary responsibility for some or all of your assets while you're alive to a person or institution (the trustee). In a trust agreement, you specify the assets that will be under control of the trust and the terms of the trust. Depending on the type of trust, you may be able to serve as your own trustee, or you and your spouse might be able to act as co-trustees, or you might have to choose another person or organization to do the job. A trustee is responsible for administering the trust, investing the trust's assets if appropriate, and distributing the trust's assets according to the terms of the trust. If the trustee is an individual, you can and should designate a successor trustee in the event of the trustee's death or inability to perform his or her duties.

IS A TRUST SIMILAR TO A WILL?

Trusts and wills have similarities, and they serve the same purpose: to transfer property to a person's beneficiaries. The differences between trusts and wills are more important than their similarities, however.

With a will, it is the responsibility of a probate court to make sure that its terms are carried out, settle any disputes that arise, and oversee the transfer of property. The terms of a will cannot be carried out until a probate judge issues an order to do so. Going through probate can take weeks, months, or even years, which delays the transfer of assets. It also requires your estate or beneficiaries to pay court fees, executor commissions, and attorney fees, and makes your will a public record.

With a trust, it is the trustee who makes sure that the terms of the trust are followed and oversees the transfer of property. Upon the death of the creator(s), the terms of the trust usually call for the trustee to immediately distribute the assets to the beneficiaries. In addition, the particulars of your estate are kept private. One caveat: Make sure you are comfortable with any fees associated with the trusts.

WHAT IS A REVOCABLE LIVING TRUST?

A revocable living trust, often referred to as a revocable trust or a living trust, is a type of trust that lets the creator make changes to the trust's assets, investments, beneficiaries, or terms—or even void the trust relationship—at any time. This is why it is called a *revocable* living trust.

WHAT ARE THE ADVANTAGES OF A REVOCABLE LIVING TRUST?

In the world of financial planning, you will seldom find an arrangement that offers the flexibility, control, and security of a revocable living trust. It is flexible, because, as I mentioned, you can change the trust's assets, investments, beneficiaries, and terms at any time. It gives you control, because you pick the assets to transfer to the trust, decide how the assets will be invested and distributed, and choose the trustee to carry out your wishes. As with other types of trusts, the creator(s) of a revocable living trust can be the trustee(s) and play an active role in the management of the trust, or designate a professional manager. Finally, as with other types of trusts, this trust offers the security of knowing your wishes will be carried out, because trusts are harder to contest than wills.

A revocable living trust is an increasingly popular estate-planning tool, because it allows you to enjoy the benefits of asset ownership knowing that your family will be able to avoid the probate process and receive its inheritance easily. In addition, it is relatively easy and inexpensive to create, and can hold all types of assets: stocks, bonds, collectibles—even a closely-held business.

A revocable living trust can offer the additional benefit of protecting its creator(s) and his or her assets while he or she is alive. To take advantage of this, you must specify, in the terms of the trust, the conditions under which a co-trustee or successor trustee can assume your authority. For example, you could specify that in the event of illness or incapacity, the co-trustee or your designated successor has the authority to administer the trust. Or you can give a co-trustee or your successor trustee more limited authority. For example, if you find yourself traveling extensively or involved in other matters, and have little time to pay attention to the day-to-day demands of your trust, you could empower a co-trustee or successor trustee to take care of certain chores, such as making sure that all interest and dividend income is promptly collected and immediately invested.

DOES A REVOCABLE LIVING TRUST INCUR ADDITIONAL TAX OBLIGATIONS?

The creator's tax liability generally remains unaffected. Income gains or losses from the assets held in the trust continue being reported on the creator's federal and state income tax returns. If you set up a revocable living trust with your spouse, the two of you can combine your federal estate tax exemptions, so you can reduce your overall estate tax. (See "How can I pass my assets to my beneficiaries without paying estate taxes?" further on for an explanation of federal estate tax exemptions.)

DOES A TRUST HAVE TO BE IN EXISTENCE FOR A CERTAIN PERIOD OF TIME TO BE VALID AT THE TIME OF THE CREATOR'S DEATH?

Ownership of your assets is shifted to the trust as soon as it is set up. So, it's never too late to establish a revocable living trust.

WHAT TYPES OF INVESTMENTS SHOULD A REVOCABLE LIVING TRUST HOLD?

People who establish estate trusts usually are thinking long term: Many years from now they want their assets passed on to their beneficiaries quickly and easily. If this is your objective, you may want to consider emphasizing growth investments, such as stocks. Historically, growth investments have appreciated over time and have helped investors produce greater wealth.

WHY SHOULD I GIVE MY CHILDREN AN APPRECIATED ASSET RATHER THAN CASH?

In short, to avoid estate taxes. For example, let's say that instead of giving your children $11,000 in cash annually (that's the maximum amount you can give to someone and not incur a gift tax), you give them mutual fund shares worth $11,000. You give them this gift every year for five years. For two children, the total value of the gifts would be $110,000. In the years before you and your spouse die, the shares double in value. By having made these gifts, your estate avoids estate taxes on $220,000 (the original share value plus appreciation). Assuming a federal estate tax rate of 55 percent, the gifts would save your estate and your spouse's up to $121,000 (55 percent x $220,000).

HOW CAN I PASS MY ASSETS TO MY BENEFICIARIES WITHOUT PAYING ESTATE TAXES?

The two most common ways to pass along or transfer assets without paying estate taxes are using the Unlimited Marital Deduction and the Unified Gift and Estate Tax Credit.

The Unlimited Marital Deduction is for married couples only. If a spouse dies and the surviving spouse inherits or assumes sole ownership of the estate, the deceased is entitled to take the Unlimited Marital Deduction on his or her estate tax return. If the surviving spouse takes this deduction on the deceased spouse's estate tax return, he or she won't have to pay estate taxes no matter how large the estate.

Unlike the Unlimited Marital Deduction, the Unified Gift and Estate Tax Credit lets you give gifts and pass assets to anyone, such as children, friends, and partners. Often referred to simply as the unified credit, the Unified Gift and Estate Tax Credit is a lifetime amount by which an individual can reduce his or her gift and estate taxes. You can use the unified credit during your lifetime to pay taxes on gifts that exceed $11,000 per person, per year. You can specify that your estate use the unified credit to avoid or limit estate taxes. Or, you can do both.

WHAT IS A CREDIT SHELTER TRUST?

A credit shelter trust, also referred to as a bypass or family trust, is one way to make sure you take advantage of your unified credit to pass assets to beneficiaries other than your spouse.

Many times, spouses have sweetheart wills in which each leaves his or her assets to the other as the surviving spouse. Other times, couples have all assets in both names. This is called joint tenancy, and it effectively leaves everything to the other as the surviving spouse. In either of these situations, the surviving spouse is allowed to take the Unlimited Marital Deduction on the deceased spouse's estate tax return, and become the sole owner of the assets without paying estate taxes.

The challenge occurs when a surviving spouse wants to pass along his or her estate without a tax burden, and the value exceeds the amount exempted by his or her unified credit. For example, let's suppose that a surviving spouse dies in 2003. She has an estate worth $1,300,000, but the unified credit only exempts $1,000,000 worth of property. The estate, then, would owe taxes on $300,000. If she and her husband (who died in 2001) had split the estate, and made a financial plan for each to pass along $650,000 worth of assets using their own unified credits, the entire estate eventually would have been passed to the beneficiaries without incurring estate taxes.

A credit shelter trust is one method a couple can use alone or in combination with the Unlimited Marital Deduction to limit or avoid estate taxes, because it ensures you take advantage of both spouses' unified credit.

You and your spouse can set up credit shelter trusts to take effect while you're still alive. Either way, however, the instructions for the credit shelter trust must be included in your wills. That is, if the trust is not established while you're alive, in your will you must specify it be set up upon your death, and your spouse must do the same. You also must specify which assets to put in the trust; it makes the most sense to transfer assets you think will further appreciate in value, so that the appreciation won't count as part of the surviving spouse's estate. Then, upon the death of either one of you, the assets you designated to be put into the credit shelter trust will be transferred, and the remaining assets will be passed directly to the surviving spouse.

If the value of the assets transferred to the credit shelter trust is less than or equal to the maximum amount exempted by the unified credit, the trust won't owe estate taxes. If the value of the assets exceeds the amount exempted, then only the difference will be taxed. In addition, by taking the Unlimited Marital Deduction, the surviving spouse won't owe taxes on the part of the estate that passes directly to him or her.

Upon the death of the second spouse, the assets in the credit shelter trust will pass outside the will to the designated beneficiaries. The assets that were transferred tax-free to the surviving spouse will be part of his or her estate, which can use the spouse's unified credit to limit or offset the estate taxes on assets passed along in his or her will.

CAN A SURVIVING SPOUSE BENEFIT FROM A CREDIT SHELTER TRUST DURING HIS OR HER LIFETIME?

In today's economic environment there are many couples who have estates greater than the amount exempted by the unified credit, but not so large or liquid that the surviving spouse could maintain his or her lifestyle if the size of the estate was reduced. A credit shelter trust can be set up for the surviving spouse to receive income from the assets in the trust. It also may specify conditions under which the surviving spouse can invade the principal, such as if the surviving spouse is outliving her assets. You and your spouse should decide if either of you want to be able to receive an income from the assets, or be able to withdraw assets from the trust. Whatever you decide should be specified in your wills.

ARE THERE LIMITATIONS ON MOVING ASSETS WITHIN A CREDIT SHELTER TRUST?

In general, the trustee has the authority to make changes in investments in the trust. It is important to note that the trustee has a fiduciary responsibility to the ultimate beneficiaries of the trust, and must abide by what is often referred to as the prudent man rule. This rule states that a trustee should act as any prudent man would with regard to the assets of the trust. As far as distributing assets from the trust prior to the death of the second spouse, that depends on the language of the trust and again is subject to the authority of the trustee.

WHAT IS A CHARITABLE REMAINDER TRUST?

A charitable remainder trust is an investment vehicle that enables you to make a charitable donation, yet maintain control over how the money is invested and retain an income from your assets for you or your heirs.

To set up a charitable remainder trust, you would establish an irrevocable trust, name one or more beneficiaries of the trust, determine when the beneficiaries are to receive the assets of the trust, and then transfer assets to the trust.

Similar to a charitable gift annuity, this trust allows you to make a donation while you are living without you or your spouse losing the income from these assets. Unlike a gift annuity, however, you can specify that this trust is to provide your heirs with an income stream. While the length of time is up to you, usually this trust is set up to provide income to those specified until they die. Then, the beneficiaries begin to profit from the assets of the trust.

Charitable remainder trusts are similar to a charitable gift annuity in another way: You get a tax deduction. The reason for this is that you are transferring ownership of the earmarked assets from you to the trust. Unlike a gift annuity, however, you as the trustee still determine how the assets are invested even though you no longer own them.

Another difference between this trust and a gift annuity is the type of assets you can select for donation. You can put land and other physical assets into a charitable remainder trust, as well as other types of securities; a gift annuity, on the other hand, requires a donation of cash or stock.

WHAT IS A CHARITABLE LEAD TRUST?

A charitable lead trust has many of the same features of a charitable remainder trust, however, the end result is different. A charitable lead trust allows for the charity to receive the income for a specified period of time or your lifetime, after which your heirs receive the assets of the trust.

MY HUSBAND AND I RECENTLY EXECUTED ESTATE PLANNING DOCUMENTS WITH OUR ATTORNEY. FOR THESE DOCUMENTS TO BE HONORED, HE TELLS US THAT WE MUST REREGISTER OUR ASSETS AND CHANGE OUR BENEFICIARIES. HOW DO I GO ABOUT MAKING THESE CHANGES?

One of the most common mistakes I have seen people make in their estate planning is to not implement the necessary asset re-registrations and beneficiary changes. Many people mistakenly believe that once they have signed their wills and the papers establishing their estate trusts that they have fully implemented the plan. This is not correct! All too often the following situation occurs.

A couple holds the majority of their assets jointly; for the remaining assets, they have designated beneficiaries, either the other spouse or another person. Then, one spouse passes away. The joint assets automatically pass to the surviving spouse and the remaining assets pass directly to the beneficiaries. So all assets pass along outside of the will.

The will, however, makes several bequests and establishes a trust. Because all assets are passed directly to a spouse or beneficiary, there are no assets to fund the bequests and trust. As a result, those who were to benefit from these do not. (Setting up a credit shelter trust as we discussed earlier, for example, will require that you retitle many of your jointly held assets.)

So, how do you make the necessary changes? Your attorney will probably prepare and send letters to all of the involved parties (brokerage companies, mutual fund companies, retirement plan administrators, and so on), but do not assume these letters are enough. Many investment firms and retirement plan administrators require that you complete their forms. In addition, you may need to provide a copy of the trust document or will. Some companies may accept photocopies of these documents, but others require originals or certified copies. You should contact each company and ask them what they require. After you have completed and submitted all of the necessary documentation, call to confirm receipt and execution of your instructions.

WHAT ARE 529 PLANS AND WHY ARE THEY RECOMMENDED FOR ESTATE PLANNING?

If you're a grandparent, aunt, uncle, or other adult—even a parent—who wants to help pay for a child's education, 529 or college savings plans are an ideal method. The 529 plans are state-sponsored savings plans that let you invest money now to pay for a child's higher education at a future date. For grandparents and others wanting to help a child, these plans offer tax and estate benefits. For parents, they offer savings and tax benefits that can help them make up for the years they didn't save.

There are two ways to invest in a 529 plan. You can contribute to a plan that is already set up for a child, or you can invest in an account you open on behalf of a child. To open this account, you'll need the child's Social Security number.

Many financial advisors recommend 529 plans because they are not included in your federal estate even though you are the owner of the account. There are two exceptions, subject to the "add-back" rule in the event of the contributor's death within five years. The first exception occurs if you contribute more than $11,000 in a year and die before the period over which you spread your contribution ends. The second occurs if a distribution to your estate is made upon your death.

HOW MUCH CAN I CONTRIBUTE TO A 529 PLAN?

Your contribution to a 529 account may be as little as $25 per beneficiary, and it may be as much as $55,000 ($110,000 per married couple) in one year of a five-year period. Whether you set up an account for an individual or contribute to an account already established, however, the tax benefits are the same (see Section 8, "Taxes").

WHAT HAPPENS IF A CHILD DOESN'T USE THE MONEY I'VE INVESTED IN A 529 PLAN?

As the owner of a 529 plan, you can choose to transfer the account to another family member—even yourself—or reclaim your contributions. If you reclaim the funds, any principal taken as a deduction will be subject to income taxes, and the interest will be subject to income taxes and a 10 percent penalty.

WHAT IS A CHARITABLE GIFT ANNUITY?

As we discuss in Section 8, "Taxes," an annuity is a contractual arrangement that is usually made between an individual and an insurance company or investment firm. The contract specifies that an individual will invest an amount of money with the firm and, in return, receive fixed payments on a regular schedule over a fixed period of time. A charitable gift annuity works in much the same way, except it is a contractual arrangement with a charity.

For many people, their overarching financial goal is to accumulate assets during their working years that will generate enough income for them to maintain their lifestyle during retirement. Once in retirement, however, some find they would like to make a donation to their favorite charity while they are alive and can see the benefits. Such a contribution in many cases, however, would reduce their income.

A charitable gift annuity can let them do both: make a donation of cash or stock, and receive a steady stream of income. In
addition, the contribution is tax-deductible, and a portion of the
income from the annuity is tax-free.

As with most investment vehicles, a charitable gift annuity
isn't for everyone. You should make sure that the amount of
income you receive is sufficient even if your situation should
change, as the agreement can't be altered. In addition, there is no
benefit to your beneficiaries: If you should die before the annuity
earns out, the charity benefits, not your heirs. The tax benefits
must be assessed on an individual basis as well. However, if
these are not issues for you, it is another way to donate to a
worthwhile cause.

CAN I DESIGNATE A BENEFICIARY ON MY NONRETIREMENT ACCOUNTS?

There is a special registration that allows you to designate a beneficiary on other accounts as well. This registration is officially
titled Transfer on Death, or TOD. An account registered TOD
would read, for example, "Jane Johnson TOD James Johnson."
Jane is the owner of the account, and James is the beneficiary.
James has absolutely no rights or power on the account until
Jane's death. Most brokerage and mutual fund companies are
currently accepting accounts with this registration. It may mean
a little extra paperwork, but this can be an effective estate planning tool.

SECTION 8

~

TAXES

7 TRUTHS ABOUT TAXES

➤ For most Americans taxes are the largest household expense

➤ It's not what you earn, it's what you keep

➤ Compounded, tax-deferred savings and retirement plans are the eighth wonder of the world

➤ Home ownership continues to be a good tax shelter

➤ Tax-advantaged investments are an excellent way to reduce taxes

➤ There's little financial benefit to overpaying or underpaying the IRS

➤ Taxes can ruin the best laid financial plans; don't ignore them

E veryone has the same question about their taxes: How can I pay less of them? Accountants make their living answering this very question based on a couple's or an individual's particular situation, but in general there are four ways to reduce your tax burden: basic tax reduction, elimination of taxes, postponement of taxes, and what is commonly referred to as income shifting.

Basic tax reduction involves finding all the standard deductions each of us is entitled to take based on our situations, such as home mortgage interest, state and local income tax payments, and real estate taxes. It is the common search that many of us point to with pride when we find another allowable item. Clustering expenses that are not deductible until we can make the total amount exceed a certain threshold is another way to reduce taxes.

The term "elimination of taxes" has a magical ring to it. There are perfectly legal ways to get rid of taxes entirely. They include investing in a state's municipal bonds, making changes to the fringe benefits you receive at your job, or donating appreciated stock to a local charity.

Another approach is to postpone taxes by investing in tax-deferred financial instruments. This strategy not only allows you to put off paying taxes, but also can significantly increase your wealth. Investments in pension plans and IRAs, for example, grow more quickly than investments that are subject to yearly taxes.

Finally, you can use income shifting, which is transferring the tax burden from people in high tax brackets (often you and your spouse) to ones in lower tax brackets (perhaps your children). One way to do this is to give assets to a child.

There are ways to structure your investments that use each of these four methods, and it is these strategies that I focus on in this section.

How can I be assured of a refund on April 15?

I seldom see more pleasure on clients' faces than when they receive a large refund from the government. In fact, some of them plan for a refund by deliberately overpaying their withholding tax.

Although an income tax refund may give you the feeling that you have beaten the system somehow, there's little financial benefit to it. When you overpay, you sacrifice the investment income that money would make. If you pay an extra $1,000 to the IRS, at the end of the year your return is $1,000. If you invest that money at 8 percent, your return is $1,080. Even if come April 15 you have to pay the IRS $1,000, you've made $80 on that money in the meantime.

Similarly, there's no financial benefit to underpaying. If you underpay, you may have to pay a large tax bill on April 15, and that can throw your budget out of kilter and may even force you to borrow money to meet the payment. One of my clients fired his accountant one April because he failed to anticipate a large amount of tax due for that year. Perhaps even worse is that under certain circumstances, you also can be penalized by the government. However, whether you overpay or underpay, the amount of taxes you owe doesn't change.

If you're intent on getting a refund, you can have your employer adjust the amount it withholds for income taxes (or, if you're self-employed, you can adjust your withholding), so that you pay more to the IRS during the year. You're better off investing that money, however, and paying the IRS on April 15 if necessary.

I'M SELF-EMPLOYED AND MY ESTIMATED TAX PAYMENTS CAN GET A LITTLE STEEP IF I'VE HAD A DOWN QUARTER. HOW CAN I AVOID THIS?

Estimated quarterly tax payments are based on your estimated income for the year, not on your quarterly income. If your quarterly income fluctuates, you should plan to pay taxes in down quarters from the income earned in good quarters.

If you anticipate that your income will be less for the upcoming year than it was for the previous year, you can adjust the amount you pay quarterly accordingly. If you estimate incorrectly, however, and your income doesn't decline and you owe the IRS money at the end of the year, you may be subject to a penalty. If you are unsure whether your income will be more or less than the previous year, the safest strategy is to pay the same amount in estimated quarterly taxes that you paid the previous year.

This way, you won't be subject to a penalty if you earn more, and you'll receive a refund if you earn less.

This is also a good strategy to use if you expect that your income will increase over the previous year, but may fluctuate quarter to quarter. That is, you can pay the same amount in estimated quarterly taxes as you did the previous year and defer payment on the increase until April 15 without penalty. In addition to avoiding higher quarterly payments, this lets you have use of your money for a longer period of time. Assuming an 8 percent return, for every $1,000 you keep from the government for six months, you will gain an extra $40 in pretax income.

IS THERE ANYTHING I CAN DO AT YEAR END TO REDUCE MY TAXES?

Yes, review your investments that are not included in your retirement accounts to see which ones throw off year-end distributions of income or capital gains. Then call the investment institution(s) and ask them what they're estimating the capital gains will be at year end. Often, even the actual amount of the gains are available before the end of the year, if you ask. By doing this, you might be able to find some losses in certain parts of your portfolio that you can use to offset the gains. And if there are no losses and only gains, then it gives you time to plan accordingly.

I JUST RECEIVED A LARGE CAPITAL GAINS DISTRIBUTION OF $4,700 ON AN INVESTMENT, EVEN THOUGH I LOST MONEY THIS YEAR. HOW CAN I AVOID TAKING TAX HITS LIKE THIS?

The short answer is, you can't, as long as you want to keep your money in a pooled investment, such as a mutual fund. If your money is invested in a diversified pool managed by a third party, you own shares of that pool just like thousands of other investors. The manager of that portfolio actively buys and sells securities during the course of the year. If securities are sold for a profit, that profit has to be distributed to the shareholders by the end of the year. Shareholders, in turn, owe capital gains taxes on their individual portion of the profit. It could be a short-term capital gain if the portfolio manager held it for less than a year, or it could be a long-term capital gain that receives favorable tax treatment because the manager held the security for more than a year.

I HAVE TO WRITE A $3,000 CHECK TO THE IRS BECAUSE OF THE INTEREST EARNINGS ON MY INVESTMENTS EVEN THOUGH I REINVEST THEM. CAN I AVOID THIS?

There are a few alternatives to taxable investments that you might consider investigating. One is tax-free municipal bonds or a professionally managed mutual fund of municipal bonds. The income that these bonds generate is exempt from federal income taxes and, in many cases, state taxes. These investments can provide you with high monthly income as well as enough diversi-fication to protect your principal. In addition, you can emphasize the quality of these bonds to help manage your risk. Investors who are taxed at a federal rate of 28 percent or higher usually keep more of their income from municipal bond investments, even if they subsequently reinvest the income in a taxable mutual fund.

Let's look at an example. On a $100,000 taxable investment hypothetically yielding 7 percent, you would earn approximately $7,000. You might keep as little as $3,900 after federal and state taxes. If that same investment was in tax-exempt bonds yielding 5 percent, you would earn and keep approximately $5,000. That's 28 percent more income.

That said, I meet many people who own tax-free bonds but shouldn't; they would keep more of what they earn if they were in an investment that required them to pay some taxes, because taxable investments can provide higher yields even after taxes. To determine if you should invest in tax-free or taxable bonds, see Section 2, "Bonds."

Another avenue you might want to explore is placing some of the dollars that are producing the taxable interest into tax-deferred accounts, such as IRAs and 401(k)s. When you turn on the income spigot at retirement, let's say age 62, you will have more income built up in your investment accounts than if you paid taxes as you go. Although you will have to pay taxes when you withdraw the money, generally you are in a lower tax bracket at retirement.

Variable annuities are another type of tax-deferred investment and have been a popular vehicle for people who want to
shelter their investment earnings from taxes. One advantage to
variable annuities is that while IRAs and 401(k)s have annual
investment limits ($3,000 and $11,000 for individuals, respectively, as of 2002), variable annuities have no such limits.

WHAT ARE VARIABLE ANNUITIES?

Let's begin by understanding annuities. An annuity is a contract
sold by a life insurance or investment firm to an individual.
Under the terms of this contract, an individual invests money
with the firm either by making payments over a period of time or
as a lump sum, and the money grows tax-deferred. In return for
a person's investment, the insurance or investment company
guarantees the investor regular payments for life. The contract
specifies the age at which payments begin, the amount, and the
payment schedule, among other things.

An insurance or investment company considers many factors
when determining the amount of your payments, such as the
amount you invest, the length of time you invest, your life
expectancy, and whether you are considering a variable or fixed
annuity. With a variable annuity, the value of your investment
affects the amount of your payments, whereas with a fixed annuity, your payments are always the same. For example, if you
invest $10,000 in a variable annuity and it grows to $15,000,
your payments will be more than if your investment shrinks to
$8,000. If you invest in a fixed annuity, on the other hand, the
payments will remain the same despite fluctuations in the value
of your investment.

Like most investments, annuities are not for everyone.
Research them or talk to your financial advisor about the pros
and cons to determine if they are a good opportunity for you.

HOW DO I KNOW IF I'M SUBJECT TO THE ALTERNATIVE MINIMUM TAX?

The alternative minimum tax is intended to keep wealthy tax-
payers from finding so many loopholes that they end up paying
too little in federal income tax. It's extraordinarily complicated to

figure, but basically, if you have so many deductions that your overall tax liability falls below about 28 percent of your income, you may be subject to the AMT. The way to determine if it applies to you is to use the worksheet on IRS Form 6251, although most computer or online tax services will figure this for you.

I AM INVESTING IN MUTUAL FUNDS FOR LONG-TERM GROWTH, BUT A LOT OF MY GAINS ARE EATEN UP BY TAXES. IS THERE ANYTHING THAT I COULD BE DOING TO REDUCE MY TAX BURDEN?

By investing in tax-managed growth funds, investors can build wealth over time and limit their tax liability. A tax-managed growth fund seeks out companies that the portfolio management team believes have excellent long-term growth potential and can remain part of the portfolio for many years.

An indicator of long-term growth potential is using profits to finance future growth rather than using them to pay dividends to shareholders. When a company does this, a portfolio manager knows that it is focused on the growth of the company. Aside from the fact that a company with a long-term strategy is a better investment than one looking to make a quick buck, such companies are particularly good for tax-managed funds because they provide growth, yet because they don't pay much if any dividends, limit investors' taxable income.

Investing in companies that are likely to remain part of the fund's portfolio for many years is another way portfolio managers help investors reduce taxes. Frequent trading of securities can generate significant capital gains that are taxed at ordinary income tax rates (rather than the lower capital gains rate). By keeping turnover to a minimum, there are no unnecessary gains.

I FEEL LIKE I AM WORKING HALF THE YEAR TO PAY MY TAXES. IS THIS REALLY THE CASE?

There is a Washington research group called the Tax Foundation that tracks how long the average American must work to pay his or her taxes, and it publishes its findings around tax time each year. According to the foundation, in 1997, the average American had to work two hours and forty-nine minutes of each eight-hour work day to make enough money to pay all federal, state and local taxes. In 1990, the tax bite stood at two hours and forty minutes. In 1960, it was two hours and twenty minutes. In 1930, it was only fifty-eight minutes. Americans now pay more in total taxes than they do for food, clothing, and housing combined. These calculations are based on all federal, state, and local taxes, not just income taxes.

WHY IS TAX-DEFERRED GROWTH SO IMPORTANT?

Deferring taxes lets the magic of compound interest work on more of your money. When your money grows in a tax-deferred investment, it is not taxed every year and has the potential to grow at a much faster rate than the same money in a taxable investment. If you were to invest $100,000 for ten years on a tax-deferred basis at a 10 percent annual rate of return, your investment would be worth about $270,704. If that same amount were invested for the same length of time in a taxable investment, it would only be worth approximately $198,978, a difference of 36 percent. (This assumes a federal tax rate of 31 percent.)

IS A HOME A GOOD TAX-SHELTERED INVESTMENT?

Although I wouldn't consider a home the best tax-sheltered investment, it does provide four important tax advantages. First, a home will generally increase in value over time and isn't subject to capital gains taxes until it is sold.

Second, new tax laws allow homeowners to pull gains out of the sale of their primary home—as much as $250,000 for individuals and $500,000 for couples—without being liable for capital gains on it.

Third, the mortgage interest costs—whether they are incurred to finance the original purchase or to finance later improvements—are tax-deductible.

Finally, your home is virtually the only nonbusiness or entirely investment-related asset that you can borrow against and for which you receive a tax deduction on that loan.

IF I TAKE A LUMP SUM OUT OF MY 401(K) FOR A DOWN PAYMENT ON A HOUSE, WHAT WOULD BE THE TAX CONSEQUENCES?

The first tax consequence of taking a cash distribution from your 401(k) is the 20 percent mandatory federal withholding. Let's say you take a distribution of $50,000. Your employer is required to withhold 20 percent of it, or $10,000.

Then, there are federal income taxes. Assuming you are in a 31 percent tax bracket, you owe an additional 11 percent, or $5,500. This leaves you with $34,500 of the original $50,000.

If you are under age 59½, the IRS imposes a 10 percent, or $5,000, penalty for early withdrawal if this is not your first house. (If it is your first house, you won't incur this penalty.) This further reduces the amount available for a down payment to $29,500, and we haven't considered any state or local taxes that you might incur.

A better option is to explore the possibility of *borrowing* the money from your 401(k). Borrowing money from a 401(k) requires that you use it for a purpose that is approved under the plan, and that you agree to pay the money back on a regular basis. Borrowing to make a down payment on a house is allowed under many 401(k) plans, and you don't incur any taxes or penalties. The downside to borrowing from a 401(k) is that if you leave the company where you're working for any reason (perhaps you change jobs or are laid off), the amount borrowed becomes payable in full.

ARE THERE ANY TAX PENALTIES IF I TAKE MY MONEY OUT OF A CD BEFORE IT MATURES?

If you withdraw money from a CD before it matures, you forfeit some interest, from one to three months' worth. There also might be early withdrawal charges imposed by the institution with which you have the CD. However, there are no tax penalties. You will be taxed on the interest, but that's not a tax penalty— whether or not you keep or terminate the CD, you must pay income taxes on the interest you earn.

WHAT'S THE POTENTIAL TAX BITE ON MY IRA IF SOMETHING WERE TO HAPPEN TO ME?

If your spouse is the beneficiary of your IRA, it could be transferred to him or her without any tax consequences. If your IRA
beneficiary isn't your spouse, the tax bite can be substantial.

If you have $200,000 in your IRA, your federal estate tax lia-
bility could be as high as 41 percent. In hard numbers, that is
$82,000 of your $200,000 going on a one-way trip to Washington.
Then, your beneficiary must pay income tax on the lump-sum
distribution. If he or she is in the 39 percent federal income tax
bracket, this amounts to $78,000.

One way to ease this tax pain is for the beneficiary to elect to
receive a series of distributions from the IRA rather than a lump
sum. The beneficiary must elect to do this within a year of the
death of the decedent. When a nonspousal beneficiary spreads
IRA distributions over his or her lifetime, it spreads the tax payments over a long period of time—almost like a "reverse tax
deferral."

DO I PAY CAPITAL GAINS TAX ON INHERITED ASSETS IF I SELL THEM RIGHT AWAY?

In most cases, you won't, or at least not very much. The value of
an inheritance is based on what the estate is worth on the decedent's most recent tax return, not what the decedent originally
paid for the property, so the capital gains are what the estate
sells for minus its value on that final tax return.

Let's say, for example, that you were to inherit an estate that
was valued at $200,000 on the decedent's most recent tax return.
As long as you immediately sell it for $200,000, it won't trigger
any capital gains tax, although you'd still have to pay income and
possibly estate taxes on it.

However, if you sell it for $300,000, then you would owe capi-
tal gains taxes on the profit of $100,000. If you wait to sell the
assets, you would owe capital gains taxes on the appreciation, if
any, from the time you inherited the assets.

MANY COMPANIES ADVERTISE A 32 PERCENT TAX SAVINGS IN THE YEAR MONEY IS INVESTED IN A TAX-SHELTERED ACCOUNT SUCH AS A 401(K) OR A 403(B). IS THIS CLAIM ACCURATE?

Yes, the claim is accurate. Here's how I and others draw this conclusion. Let's assume this year you earn $50,000 and contribute $1,000 to your 401(k). At the end of the year, your W-2 will show $49,000 in earned income, because 401(k) and 403(b) contributions are deducted from your total earnings for tax purposes. Therefore, your taxable income for that tax year is $1,000 less than you actually earned.

Assuming also that you are in the 28 percent federal and 4 percent state tax brackets, it is reasonable to conclude that by contributing $1,000 to your tax-sheltered account, you have reduced your taxes by 32 percent for a savings of $320. We can further look at this as a 32 percent return on your money regardless of the investment you chose to own in the 401(k) plan.

There is another way to look at this. Of the $1,000 that you contribute to your tax-sheltered account, $680 was your own contribution and the government subsidized the additional $320 through tax savings from the creation of the 401(k). This $680 of your own money and the $320 subsidy from the government equals the $1,000 contribution. Similar math would apply to a tax-exempt contribution to an IRA.

IS THE NEW YORK STATE COLLEGE SAVINGS PROGRAM ONLY FOR PEOPLE WHO LIVE IN NEW YORK, OR CAN I TAKE ADVANTAGE OF IT AS SOMEONE WHO WORKS IN NEW YORK AND PAYS NEW YORK INCOME TAXES?

Most states offer these plans, which are called 529 plans after Section 529 of the Internal Revenue Code. Many work in basically the same way, so let's use the New York program as an example. This program benefits more than people who live in New York; it benefits everyone who pays income tax to the State of New York, which includes people who live in another state but commute to and work in New York City or any other city in New York State. (There are many state-sponsored 529 plans that have no residency requirements. If your state doesn't have a plan, consider looking into one of these.)

If you pay taxes to New York State, you can deduct the full amount of your contribution from your New York State taxable income, up to $5,000 per year per person. For couples, the maximum deduction is $10,000 per year.

Anyone who is interested in building a college savings fund for a child can establish this account. You can establish this account for your own child, or a child of a relative or friend. You can contribute regular investments of as little as $25 by using your bank's electronic funds transfer service.

The investment management of the New York college savings program is administered by several nationally recognized financial services firm. You should find out the name of the management firm for the 529 plan you're considering and investigate its track record. In all plans, however, the investments will be in a combination of equities, bonds, and money market instruments, and will be allocated depending on how close the youngster is to attending college. That is, if the child will attend college in a year or two, the portfolio selections will be more conservative than if the child is a toddler.

WHAT ARE THE TAX ADVANTAGES OF 529 PLANS?

Whether you set up an account for an individual or contribute to an already-existing account, the tax benefits are the same, and as follows:

*   Contributions that do not exceed $11,000 per year ($22,000 if filing jointly), or $55,000 in one year of a five-year period ($110,000 if filing jointly), are exempt from the federal gift tax as long as you don't give additional gifts to this individual during the corresponding time period. For example, the IRS would treat a $55,000 contribution as if you were giving this individual $11,000 per year for five years. Therefore, any other gifts you made to this individual within the five-year period might result in a federal gift tax liability.
*   Some 529 or college savings plans allow you to deduct your contribution from your state income taxes if you are investing in a plan that is sponsored by the state in which you are a resident. As noted in the previous question, in New York State an individual resident can deduct a contribution of up to $5,000 per year; a couple can deduct a contribution of up to

$10,000 per year. No plan allows you to deduct contributions from your federal income taxes.

*   Monies in a 529 plan earn interest on a tax-deferred basis. The interest is subject to state income taxes when it is withdrawn, but it is exempt from federal income taxes from 2002 until 2011 if you make a qualified withdrawal.

A *qualified withdrawal* is a withdrawal made to pay qualified expenses at a qualified institution. Qualified expenses include tuition, room and board, fees, books, supplies, and services for special-needs students. Qualified institutions are schools that have a Federal School Code. They include: accredited public and private colleges and universities; graduate and postgraduate programs; most community colleges; and some trade and vocational schools. To determine if a school has a Federal School Code, go to www.fafsa.ed.gov on the Web.

If the monies in a college savings account are used for purposes other than higher education expenses, there is a federally mandated 10 percent penalty that is imposed on the earnings. In addition, the tax-free withdrawals would not apply if the money is not used for higher education. The money in a 529 plan is the asset of the beneficiary, although the selected owner controls the money and who the beneficiary is. These plans have exploded in popularity over the last several years as most major money management firms have developed relationships with a selected state.

As a financial planner I feel it is important to remind you to remember the rule, "Never let the tax tail wag the investment dog." Carefully consider the investment portfolios the management firm implements (you do not have a choice of portfolios) alongside the tax benefits before making your decision.

AT THE END OF THE YEAR, I MAKE CASH DONATIONS TO SEVERAL CHARITIES. THIS YEAR, MY ACCOUNTANT RECOMMENDED I DONATE SOME OF MY APPRECIATED STOCK RATHER THAN CASH. HOW DOES THIS HELP ME?

If you are considering selling some stock and taking the profits, *and* you are also planning to make a charitable donation, it can be advantageous to make a donation of stock, rather than sell the stock and donate cash. The reason for this is that the profit you make on the sale of your stock will be taxed. A charity that is tax-exempt, however, can sell that stock without paying taxes. Let's look at an example.

Suppose some years ago you bought 100 shares of stock at $25 per share. The price has since doubled to $50, so you want to take your profit of $2,500. Also, you're planning to donate $2,500 to your favorite charity.

If you sell your stock, you'll have to pay capital gains on your profit of $2,500. Assuming you are in the 20 percent tax bracket, you'll have $2,000 to donate after taxes. If you were to donate 50 shares instead, however, you could claim a $2,500 deduction. And because the charity is tax-exempt, it could sell your stock and benefit from the entire $2,500. You can then sell the other 50 shares to recoup your original investment.

Donating stock also can be beneficial to a charity if the charity doesn't need the cash right away. It can opt to hold onto the stock anticipating it will appreciate in value and benefit from the dividends, if any, in the meantime. Then, the charity can sell the stock down the road when it needs the cash.

Do I HAVE TO OWN STOCK FOR A CERTAIN PERIOD OF TIME BEFORE I DONATE IT IN ORDER TO TAKE A TAX DEDUCTION?

As long as you itemize you can take a tax deduction, but the amount can change. If you own stock for less than one year and donate it to charity, your tax deduction will be the fair market value less appreciation. If you donate stock you've owned for more than one year, your tax deduction will be equivalent to the market value.

Let's suppose you purchased 300 shares of a company at $10 per share, for a total investment of $3,000. Nine months later, the stock had risen to $15 per share; thirteen months later the stock was at $17 per share. If you donated the stock after owning it for nine months, your tax deduction would be $3,000. However, if you waited and donated it at thirteen months, your tax deduction would be $5,100.

ARE THERE ANY TAX ADVANTAGES TO GIVING DEPRECIATED STOCK TO MY BENEFICIARIES OR TO CHARITIES?

There's little advantage to giving heirs depreciated stock, because heirs can't inherit losses. For example, if you purchased a stock at $40 per share and it is $20 per share today, you could sell it and take a loss of $20 per share on your taxes to offset capital gains or income. If you should die when the stock is at $20 per share, however, your heirs cannot use the difference of $20 per share to reduce their taxes. If they inherit the stock at $20 per share, however, and while they own it the stock dips further to $10 per share, they can take the loss of $10 per share on their taxes. Therefore, generally speaking, it's advisable for individuals to take their own losses. Against capital gains, each dollar of loss can offset a dollar of gain; up to $3,000 of losses can be used to offset regular income.

If you have losses in your portfolio and are considering making a donation to a charity, it's more advantageous tax-wise to sell the stocks and donate the cash. The reason for this is twofold. First, you can use the loss you incur by selling your stock to offset your income or capital gains taxes. Second, you can take a charitable deduction for your cash donation.

I UNDERSTAND THE ADVANTAGES OF GIVING STOCK, RATHER THAN CASH, TO CHARITIES. I OWN MUTUAL FUNDS, HOWEVER, AND NOT INDIVIDUAL STOCKS. CAN I DONATE MUTUAL FUND SHARES?

Yes, most mutual fund companies allow investors to donate shares. You can look on the Web site of your mutual fund company for the details and necessary forms, or you can call and have the information and forms mailed to you. Usually, a mutual fund company specifies a minimum donation, and requires both you and the charity to complete the corresponding sections of the form. However, the process is relatively quick and painless.

WHAT IS THE ADVANTAGE OF HAVING CHARITABLE CONTRIBUTIONS DEDUCTED FROM MY PAYCHECK BY MY EMPLOYER RATHER THAN MAKING THE DONATIONS DIRECTLY?

The advantage to making charitable donations in this manner is that many employers have established programs whereby they will contribute a percentage of their employee's donations to charities, or they will match donations dollar for dollar. So, making charitable donations through such programs benefits your favorite charities. However, there is no additional tax benefit.

I MADE A DONATION TO A TAX-EXEMPT ORGANIZATION ONLY TO BE TOLD BY MY ACCOUNTANT THAT MY CONTRIBUTION WASN'T TAX-DEDUCTIBLE. HOW CAN THAT BE?

The IRS grants many organizations tax-exempt status, which means that they are exempt from paying federal income tax. However, contributions to tax-exempt organizations are not necessarily deductible.

To be tax-deductible, a contribution must be made to an organization granted tax-exempt status under Section 501(c)(3) of the tax code. Qualified organizations include nonprofit groups that are: religious, charitable, educational, scientific, or literary, or work to prevent cruelty to children or animals; war veterans' organizations; and organizations run by local, state, or federal government for a public purpose, such as the police or fire departments.

Many organizations are granted tax-exempt status under Sections 501(c)(4), 501(c)(5), and other sections of the tax code. Examples of such groups include civic leagues, social and sports clubs, labor unions, homeowners associations, and political groups. While these groups do not have to pay income tax, contributions to them are not deductible.

If you do not know the tax-exempt status of an organization, you should ask the organization's leader or check with your local IRS office.

SECTION 9

~

FINANCIAL PLANNING

7 STEPS TO A FINANCIAL PLAN

➤ Get your spouse or significant other involved

➤ Obtain referrals to certified financial planners

➤ Set up initial consultations with at least three planners

➤ Determine if the planners' recommendations will be unbiased and independent

➤ Ask the planners for references and call them

➤ Look for a planner until you find one who has a philosophy and belief system you can embrace

➤ Hire a planner that communicates to you aggressively and often

C reating a financial plan can be an intimidating prospect, so much so that many people don't even start, much less complete one. Rather, they focus for years on only one or two aspects of their finances—investing and taxes being the more popular ones. To do this, however, can be self-defeating. As we've seen in previous sections, you can work, save, and invest for a lifetime only to lose much of what you've earned to capital gains taxes; you can select investments that limit your tax liability only to be adversely affected by the limited long-term growth of your assets; and you can will your assets to your beneficiaries only to have them sell their inheritances to pay estate taxes.

Often times, people don't create a plan because they think of it as setting their finances and future in stone. In fact, the opposite is true. As your circumstances change, you should reevaluate your plan and make sure it's still right for you. On the other hand, a plan can deter you from reacting to the moment and making a mistake you'll long live to regret. Reviewing your long-term plan is one of the best cures I know for market jitters.

Another reason people avoid planning is the amount of work and time it takes. Initially, this is true. Once you have a plan in place, however, you'll immediately notice that it takes less work and time to maintain your plan than it did to tend to your finances previously. It also eliminates much worry.

If you don't have a financial plan and don't know where to start, can't face the thought of creating one, or don't have the time, consider hiring a Certified Financial Planner. A CFP can make the process proceed more quickly and easily. Perhaps even more important, an advisor can bring perspective developed by years of experience, and help you maintain your plan, reevaluate it, and alter it as needed.

WHAT CAN A FINANCIAL ADVISOR DO FOR ME?

A financial advisor can work with you to help reduce your taxes, set aside resources to put the kids through college, handle a sudden inheritance, or plan a comfortable retirement. In short, the role of a financial advisor is to help you meet your financial goals.

At the outset, the financial advisor you choose should try to obtain a complete financial picture of you: your past lifestyle, goals, and investments, as well as your current monthly income, expenses, objectives, and investments. The advisor should then provide you with an accurate overview of your financial situation, and recommend a realistic and objective course of action based on your financial goals and resources.

Once you have a strategy, your advisor should make specific investment recommendations. He or she can help you decide how much to invest, which investments—such as stocks, bonds, and mutual funds—to choose, and which investment vehicles—such as IRAs, 401(k)s, and annuities—are best for your needs. Your advisor also should analyze your debt and make recommendations for how you can pay down your most expensive credit, while making better use of your inexpensive loans.

A professional financial advisor's job does not end there. You should feel that you can always ask your advisor, "How am I doing?" He or she should be constantly monitoring your financial strategy and portfolio to ensure that they remain current. Changes in the economy might make it wise to rethink your strategy or how it's being implemented, as could a change in your job or family status. While your advisor can monitor the former, he or she can't know the latter unless you convey it. So, it is as important for you to keep your advisor up to date as it is for him or her to update you.

As part of monitoring your portfolio, your advisor should continually evaluate the performance of your investments and discuss with you the results, including how each one compares to the appropriate benchmark. While your advisor cannot predict or influence your investment results, he or she should help you judge your progress and determine if any changes are warranted to reach your financial goals.

While working with an advisor, you should expect him or her to make clear and specific recommendations, and explain his or her reasoning in terms that you can understand. In the case of mutual funds, the advisor should have confidence in the management of any investment he or she recommends, plus knowledge about the current portfolio strategy. In addition, an advisor should say what are the realistic risks and rewards of each investment. Every investment choice has strengths and weaknesses compared to the alternatives. You should never walk away feeling that you only have half the story.

The most valuable service that an advisor can provide is to help you stay the course with your investment program. Staying the course does not necessarily mean staying put, however. Rather, expect your financial advisor to recommend adjustments to your asset allocation in response to any meaningful change in your lifestyle, priorities, assets, or responsibilities.

Beyond these basics, many investors could use more specialized assistance in a range of areas, such as advice on retirement-plan distribution options, setting up and servicing retirement plans for small businesses, or estate planning. A financial planner often can be of great assistance with these needs as well.

HOW DO I FIND A FINANCIAL ADVISOR?

Begin by asking for referrals from friends and trusted professionals. Your accountant or attorney should already have an understanding of your financial resources and the financial challenges that you may face in the future. One of them may be able to make a recommendation.

Another way to find a financial planner would be to attend advisors' free seminars or read advisors' free newsletters; advisors commonly offer these at no cost to potential clients. At the very least, seminars and newsletters expose you to the knowledge levels of the advisors, their communication skills, and most importantly, their beliefs and methods of solving clients' financial problems.

There are general resources to tap as well. You can call the Financial Planning Association (FPA) (1-800-945-4237) or access its Web site (www.fpanet.org) for a list of Certified Financial Planners in your area.

I HAVE SET UP AN INITIAL MEETING WITH A FINANCIAL PLANNER. WHAT ARE SOME OF THE QUESTIONS THAT I SHOULD ASK?

The first question you should ask—even before you set up your first appointment with a financial planner—is whether or not there is a charge for the initial consultation. Many top planners won't charge for an initial visit, since they're more interested in building a long-term relationship. Others will charge as much as

$500. If you're going to pay a fee for a consultation, make sure that he or she comes highly recommended.

Once you have arranged a consultation, your initial meeting should serve three purposes: to learn about the planner, to understand how he or she operates, and to find out how he or she communicates. It is best to arrive at this meeting prepared with a list of questions. Here are some that can help you learn about the planner's background and experience:

- How long has he or she been practicing?
- Where did he or she practice previously?
- What is his or her education?
- Does he or she have other credentials (such as an MBA or CPA)?
- How many clients does he or she have?
- Is he or she registered with the SEC?
- Is he or she familiar with your specific issues?
- Does he or she have experience working with people in situations similar to your own, or who have similar requirements? For example, if your primary interest is retirement planning, ask the planner if she or he has expertise in this area.
- Can he or she provide names of clients to call as references?

It is also important to understand how the planner operates. Some planners only give advice, and you are then responsible for carrying out the investment decisions on your own. Others will not only give you advice but are prepared to manage your investments on an on-going basis. You should determine in the first meeting whether there is a fit between your needs and the planner's style. To do this, here are some additional questions you should ask the planner:

- Who will be your primary contact at the firm?
- Who will monitor your portfolio?
- Is he or she available for phone calls during the day?
- How is he or she compensated?
- Does he or she sell any products?
- How does he or she stay in contact with clients?

As the planner answers your questions, you can determine whether you are comfortable with the way he or she communicates. Remember, financial planning is a very personal business. You want someone with whom you can talk to with ease, so ask all the questions that are on your mind.

How should I check my planner's references?

Before I answer this question, I'll note that it's best to have many references whom you can contact as opposed to only a few. A long list lets you choose which references to call, and how many.

If a planner doesn't have a ready list of references and asks who you'd like to speak with, you could ask for the names of former clients, or you could ask for a specific person, such as whomever the advisor met with right before you sat down in the office. Once you have a list of people to call, the next step is making a list of questions to ask them. Some typical questions to ask a reference are:

- How many years have you been working with this financial advisor?
- Were you referred to this planner, or did you come to hire him or her another way?
- How have your assets performed since you have been working with this advisor?
- How accessible is the advisor when you need him or her for financial advice?
- Does he or she explain his or her recommendations to your satisfaction?
- How often does he or she contact you and send statements?
- Is the advisor proactive in monitoring your plan and investments, and making recommendations?

What kind of credentials should a financial planner have?

Most financial planners have a four-year college degree in a discipline, such as accounting, economics, or finance, that is naturally tied to financial planning. Beyond that, there are several noncollegiate educational programs that provide a thorough grounding in all areas of financial planning. Most prominent are the courses offered by the College for Financial Planning and the Financial Planning Association. Taking such courses is the first step towards earning the Certified Financial Planner, or CFP, designation.

The next step is passing a demanding series of examinations given by the CFP Board (originally called the International Board of Standards and Practices for Certified Financial Planners). These exams cover investments, tax management, insurance, employee benefits, retirement planning, and estate planning. In addition, individuals must meet work experience requirements and meet ethical standards to receive the designation.

After you become a CFP, you must continue your education to maintain this designation. I believe that if an individual has made a commitment to a career or a profession in financial planning, he or she should have, or should be pursuing, a professional designation that goes along with serving in that profession.

In addition to being a CFP, some financial advisors are accountants, lawyers, or MBAs. Following are some of the more esoteric designations you might encounter:

- **PFS (Personal Financial Specialist):** Issued to CPAs who have experience in financial planning and who pass an exam offered by the American Institute of CPAs.
- **CFA (Chartered Financial Analyst):** Primarily held by institutional money managers and stock analysts who have the required work experience and have passed a series of tests.
- **CLU (Chartered Life Underwriter):** Held mostly by life-insurance agents, who have signed a code of ethics, have three years' experience in the field, and have completed ten college-level courses.
- **ChFC (Chartered Financial Consultant):** Same as the CLU, with some additional course work required.

IS THERE A WAY TO FIND OUT IF AN ADVISOR HAS ANY BLACK MARKS AGAINST HIM?

Several regulatory agencies police the investment industry and provide such information. One is the SEC. It maintains what is called a CRD, or Central Record Depository, which is sort of a file of brokers' rap sheets. To receive information in this file, send a letter to SEC Operations Center, Freedom of Information Act, 6432 General Green Way, Alexandria, VA 22312. In your letter, specifically request to be notified of all complaints or investigations that have been filed with the SEC about a particular company or individual.

Another agency is the National Association of Securities Dealers (NASD), a self-regulatory organization that polices the securities business. Its information number is 1-800-289-9999. You may request a report on an individual or company from the NASD by phone, and it will be sent to you via e-mail or U.S. mail at no charge.

Both of these agencies can tell you if the advisor with whom you are interested in beginning a financial relationship has had complaints or violations filed against him or her, and the nature of them.

You also can contact the State Banking Department, if there is one for the state in which you reside. They regulate and police the activities of the investment advisors that operate within their state.

WHAT IS THE BEST WAY TO PAY FOR A FINANCIAL PLANNER'S SERVICES?

There is no one best method of compensation. Planners are normally compensated in one of three ways. The first is through fees, which are generally based on the value of your assets under their management or an hourly rate. Fee-only planners generally do not accept commissions, which—any fee-only planner will be happy to tell you—insulates them from conflicts of interests when they make decisions about what their clients should be buying.

The second method is through fees and commissions. Fees are charged as above, and additionally, the planner may earn commissions on the financial products that you buy.

The third method of compensation is commission-only. Many financial planners are compensated solely on the basis of commissions from the insurance and investment products that they sell as part of a financial plan. The advantage to this is that you pay only for the specific investment products you buy. I would suggest that you approach the three methods with an open mind and decide which one best fits your needs.

AFTER I PUT A FINANCIAL PLAN IN PLACE, HOW WILL I KNOW IF IT REMAINS APPROPRIATE FOR ME?

No financial plan is forever. Financial planning is an ongoing process and should reflect your changing needs and goals. Let me tell you about a few individuals who failed to recognize the need to reevaluate, or failed to reevaluate fully, their financial plans and options.

By the time their children were in college, John and Mary Z. had most of their money invested in tax-free mutual funds and were pleased about keeping their tax bills low. Then, after the kids graduated and were on their own, John and Mary retired. Now they were in a lower tax bracket, and the tax advantages of tax-free funds were no longer worth the lower rate of return. They could have generated higher after-tax returns by investing those same assets in many kinds of taxable investments. John and Mary didn't know this, however, because they failed to re-evaluate their financial plan. They misinterpreted the advantages of tax-free mutual funds and missed out on some very good investments.

One more example: After her husband died, Mrs. P. wanted to be sure that when she died, her daughter would have immediate access to all of her assets without the delay and expense of probate and estate taxes. To achieve this, Mrs. P. was careful to maintain joint registration with her daughter on all her major assets. But Mrs. P.'s plan didn't go far enough. When Mrs. P. died, her daughter quickly learned that while the joint registration provided her with immediate access to some of her assets, the majority of her mother's assets were still considered part of her estate and subject to estate tax. The estate tax may have been reduced or eliminated had Mrs. P. reevaluated her financial plan after the death of her husband and explored the use of trusts and other strategies.

WHAT DOCUMENTS SHOULD I RECEIVE FROM MY PLANNER ON A MONTHLY, QUARTERLY, OR YEARLY BASIS?

Most planners will send out, either by request or automatically, a quarterly update, which reflects the status of your portfolio. You should receive a tax report (a copy of which is sent to your accountant) each winter, as well as a complete picture of your overall financial health either annually or whenever you request one. If for some reason there are other documents you need, such as if you have real estate holdings, your advisor should offer to send them to you on a regular basis.

I WORKED OUT A RETIREMENT SAVINGS PLAN WITH A FINANCIAL ADVISOR SEVERAL YEARS AGO. I AM SATISFIED WITH THE PERFORMANCE OF MY INVESTMENTS AND FEEL I AM ON MY WAY TO A SECURE RETIREMENT. WHAT ELSE CAN A FINANCIAL ADVISOR DO FOR ME?

After you develop a flexible, long-range investment plan, your planner can help you monitor your progress and suggest adjustments as needed to meet your goals. For example, your planner may recommend changes to your retirement investments as you get older and approach retirement, or as the market shifts. Your planner also can advise how best to maintain your plan when your daily circumstances change. For example, if you or your spouse changes jobs, your planner can help you assess the retirement benefits offered or deal with an increase or decrease in income. If you or your spouse receives an inheritance or decides to divorce, your planner can offer guidance and alternatives, as he or she can when you're trying to plan your estate.

Another aspect of an advisor's job is to make sure you understand what can go wrong with your investments during a market downturn. By being informed, you may be much less likely to panic and sell at the wrong times, such as during a short-term market correction. So remember to contact your financial advisor and communicate your situation on a regular basis. By maintaining a long-term, ongoing relationship, you are more likely to retire with a lifestyle that meets your expectations.

I HANDLE ALL THE FINANCES IN MY HOUSEHOLD. WHAT DOES MY SPOUSE NEED TO KNOW IN THE EVENT THAT SHE HAS TO ACT ALONE?

Reviewing the household finances with your spouse can help protect your family's financial security in the future and give you peace of mind today. Your spouse should know the answers to these important questions:

- **What assets and liabilities do we have?** Make a list of all of your assets including securities, real estate, artwork, retirement benefits, brokerage and bank accounts, and insurance policies. Also list all debts, such as mortgages and outstanding loans, providing sufficient information about each item, including the companies and institutions involved; who holds title to the assets; and account, loan, credit card, and policy numbers. Making a complete and detailed list will let either spouse access the assets or contact the creditors easily.

- **Who are our professional advisors?** Provide your spouse with the names, addresses, and telephone numbers of your lawyer, accountant, banker, broker, and insurance agent, and any other professional advisors who you use. Your spouse should join you when you meet with your advisors to become acquainted with them and to share in any decisions that you make.

- **What financial or estate planning arrangements do we have in place?** Review your wills, trusts, insurance policies, and other arrangements with your spouse. Make sure that they are appropriate for your needs and that they are up to date. You may need to have your wills amended or redrafted if you and your spouse have moved to a different state, have gained or lost a family member, or have acquired substantial assets since your wills were last revised.

- **Where do we keep our important papers?** Your spouse needs to know where to find documents such as wills, trusts, birth certificates, marriage licenses, military records, stock and bond certificates, deeds to homes and property, and titles to automobiles. It is advisable that you keep these papers in a secure place such as a safe deposit box and that you keep copies at home or at your attorney's office. You also might want to include your list of assets and liabilities with these papers.

IS IT COMMON TO HAVE A CONTRACT WITH A FINANCIAL PLANNER. IF SO, WHAT SHOULD IT COVER?

Most financial advisors offer a standard contract to new clients, specifying what they are and are not responsible for. The agreement should clearly articulate the fees for the advisors' services as well as services that will be provided. Importantly, the agreement should allow the client (you) to terminate the relationship without penalty as well as maintain some flexibility for the advisor to terminate the relationship.

AS A WOMAN, WHAT CAN I DO TO PREPARE FOR A SECURE FINANCIAL FUTURE?

Women now have, and will continue to play, a larger role as managers of money. Statistics show that women will outlive their spouses by about seven years, and 90 percent of all women will need to be responsible for their own finances at some point in their lives. The following is a list of things that you can do to prepare for a secure financial future:

- **Recognize the benefits of starting your financial plan early.** The sooner you begin investing, the greater your chances of riding out market volatility, and the more time you will have to accumulate wealth.
- **Develop reasonable expectations.** Decide what you would like to achieve with your investment dollars and within what time frame.
- **Seek professional advice.** Most women investors are generally more willing than men to do research and educate themselves about investments. If the investment jargon you encounter doesn't make sense, ask for explanations. You should never invest without understanding the potential benefits, risks, and expenses associated with a particular investment product.
- **Adopt sound strategies.** Women tend to be more risk-averse investors than men, investing less than half as much in equities as male investors. Be sure to protect your purchasing power by maintaining some investment with growth potential. To help guard against market risk, diversify your portfolio among a variety of different types of investment products. This may help reduce your exposure to risk, as different markets rarely move in tandem.

***I AM 45 YEARS OLD AND WANT TO START PLANNING FOR MY
RETIREMENT. HAVE I LOST A LOT BY WAITING THIS LONG TO START?***

As I've mentioned elsewhere, the sooner you begin to invest, the greater your chances of riding out market volatility and the more time you will have to accumulate wealth through the magic of compound interest. If you had invested $250 each month in an investment earning an average annual return of just 6 percent starting at age 35, you would have $244,883 by the time you reached 65. If you begin that identical investment plan now, just 10 years later, you will accumulate only $113,943 by age 65. A 10-year difference in investing time amounts to $130,140 less.

Perhaps the most important thing at this point is to be realistic. Develop reasonable expectations both in terms of how much money you can put away and how much you will earn on your investments. Overestimating either of these only will lead to disappointment down the road.

***MY DAUGHTER AND SON-IN-LAW HAVE TWO YOUNG CHILDREN. I
WORRY THAT WITH THEIR EVERYDAY EXPENSES BEING SO HIGH, THEY
AREN'T SAVING FOR COLLEGE. AM I RIGHT TO BE CONCERNED?***

Yes, there's reason to be concerned. The average cost of attending a four-year college has doubled in the past ten years. The yearly tuition increases have outpaced both inflation and the growth of family income. Financial aid is not an option for everyone, and the competition for the financial aid that is available has become increasingly tougher. Low-interest student loans are available, but sizable loan balances can be quite a burden to young college graduates as they try to establish financial independence—or to their older parents (who sometimes assume responsibility for paying off these loans) as they near retirement.

In short, the best time to start saving for a child's college education was yesterday. However, establishing an early savings program can require a certain amount of discipline and sacrifice that young parents often find difficult. Most people I know get a late start, because there is little money left over to save after the bills have been paid.

Because saving enough for a college education for a child is such a challenging goal to reach today, most people should try to put aside 15 to 20 percent of their income. Just as important as the amount of money saved are the methods used to put this money to work. The higher interest-bearing accounts will provide protection against the ravages of taxes and inflation. And just a small amount invested monthly can grow to a sizable sum over the years due to compounding interest.

There are several investment vehicles available today that let relatives and others invest money for a child's college education. If this is of interest to you, you should look into college savings plans (also known as 529 plans), trusts, and custodial accounts.

I WOULD LIKE TO INVEST MORE TOWARD RETIREMENT. DO YOU HAVE SUGGESTIONS FOR HOW I CAN SAVE MORE MONEY?

By acknowledging you should be saving more money, you have already taken the crucial first step. The second step is putting your money to work for you and reinvesting the income from those investments to take advantage of the effects of compounding interest over time. Here are some suggestions to help you:

- **Contribute to a retirement plan.** If your employer provides a tax-deferred retirement plan, such as a 401(k), take advantage of it. Your contribution can be deducted directly out of your paycheck, which many people find the easiest way to save: If they don't receive the money, they don't miss it. If your employer does not offer a tax-deferred retirement plan, investigate the automatic investment plans that are offered by many investment companies. For as little as $50 per quarter, you may be able to make regular investments directly from your checking account.
- **Reduce your debt.** Many people carry high balances on their credit cards at high interest rates. Look for ways to consolidate your credit card debt at lower rates and then cut down on credit card purchases. The ideal situation is to pay off any balances on your credit cards every month so you don't incur any finance charges.
- **Spend less.** Saving an extra few dollars here and there may not sound like much of a plan, but it can add up over the course of several years. Consider this: If you save the $1 that you spend on your way to work getting a cup of coffee ($240

per year), and invest it for 30 years at a 12 percent return, you would have nearly $58,000 for your retirement.

I asked some friends what they do to cut down on expenses. One told me that she takes advantage of the resources her local library offers. Along with free books, many libraries offer free story times and other special programs for children, and free computer time. They also often offer free seminars for adults on topics ranging from financial and retirement planning to bird watching and psychic phenomenon. Fun activities don't necessarily have to be expensive.

Another friend brings lunch from home. Not only does it cost much less than buying lunch, but it is also generally healthier, with less calories and less fat. Another friend guards against impulse purchases. When he goes shopping, he always takes a list and sticks to it. When shopping for food, he never shops hungry, which helps avoid impulse food purchases. Still, not buying on impulse can be a challenge. So he even leaves the store if necessary.

Finally, several people mentioned that they clip and redeem coupons for items that they normally buy anyway.

I find most people admit that there are ways they can reduce expenses and save an extra $5 or $10 a week if they're willing to make a few, small lifestyle changes.

SHOULD I WORRY ABOUT PROTECTING MY ASSETS FROM INFLATION?

Every study I have seen lately concludes that a 65-year-old has at least 15 to 20 years ahead of them for which they need to plan so as to maintain the same lifestyle. If you believe that prices will continue to rise, then it follows that earning a real rate of return after taxes and inflation should be a fundamental investment goal. In 1973, a first class postage stamp was eight cents. In 2003, it is 37 cents. That represents more than a 350 percent increase in the cost of first class postage over 30 years.

The key to addressing this risk of extinction of your purchasing power is locating investment plans that can provide predictable income streams that grow with rising prices. For example, the oldest mutual fund in America, Massachusetts Investor Trust, established in 1924, has a 79-year track record of never missing a quarterly dividend payment, even through the Great Depression. In addition, its income stream has grown over time, allowing investors to maintain their purchasing power. Many successful large companies in America have a history of rising dividends. The S&P 500 has quadrupled its dividends over the past 23 years. So, if you were receiving $100 in dividends for the S&P 500 23 years ago, you would be receiving over $500 in dividends today.

INFLATION HASN'T BEEN VERY HIGH RECENTLY, SO HOW MUCH OF A DIFFERENCE COULD IT MAKE IN MY RETIREMENT PLANS?

When I'm speaking before an audience, I usually demonstrate the effects of inflation over time by asking, "How many of you have spent more money buying your most recent car than you spent buying your first home?" Most people in the audience raise their hands. Very simply put, over the past twenty years, inflation has averaged almost 6 percent per year. If inflation continues to grow at that average rate, 25 years from now, a dollar could be worth just 22 cents. It would take $4.19 to buy the same items that a dollar would buy today.

I HAVE SEVERAL PROFESSIONAL ADVISORS—AN ACCOUNTANT, ATTORNEY, INSURANCE AGENT, AND A FINANCIAL PLANNER. THE AREAS ON WHICH THEY ADVISE OVERLAP. HOW CAN I MAKE SURE THE WORK EACH IS DOING IS COMPLEMENTING, AND NOT NEGATING, THE WORK OF ANOTHER?

One thing that a financial advisor will often do is work as a quarterback with your team of professionals. His or her work will involve every corner that your other pros are handling: your estate, your insurance, your annual tax bill, and so on. No one is better positioned to oversee their efforts than your financial advisor. If you ask your financial advisor to ensure that everyone is working toward the same goals—and make sure your other professionals are willing to work with him or her—you shouldn't have any problems.

***I'M CONSIDERING CHANGING FINANCIAL PLANNERS. HOW SHOULD I GO
ABOUT MOVING FROM ONE PLANNER TO ANOTHER? WHAT DOCUMENTS
DO I NEED AND WILL IT IMPACT MY INVESTMENTS?***

If there's one thing that financial planners are familiar with, it's
keeping paperwork in order. So all of what you need is with your
planner. Your main concern in this situation is making sure
you're aware of every piece of your finances—everything in your
portfolio, your 401(k), IRA, all forms of insurance, and so on—
and that your new planner is aware of them, too. You don't want
something to be lost in the shuffle. Your current planner should
provide you with documentation that has a complete itemization
of all your assets under his or her management, as well as the
institutions they are with, account numbers, and value. You
would then provide this information to your new advisor. Your
investments need not be disrupted.

The more important question is why you're switching planners. If there was something your planner did that you were
unhappy with, make sure your new advisor is aware of your concerns and plans to proceed in a direction more to your liking.

***I HEARD ABOUT A BROKER STEALING $3 BILLION OF HIS CLIENTS'
MONEY. WHAT KIND OF PROTECTION DO I HAVE THAT MY BROKER OR
FINANCIAL PLANNER DOESN'T EMBEZZLE MONEY FROM ME AND MY
FAMILY?***

What I have found in my eighteen years as a financial planner is
that the source of many such problems are people who represent
themselves as brokers and financial advisors but who do not hold
the necessary licenses. They act as financial advisors, but they
are not subject to regulation because, without a license, they
aren't on the regulators' radar screens. Therefore, the first way to
protect yourself is to make sure your broker or planner has the
proper licenses. You can do this by calling the Financial Planning
Association (1-800-945-4237), or the NASD (1-800-289-9999),
which have records of all licensed financial advisors.

There are two different regulatory organizations that you can
categorize as "securities police." Their primary job is to protect
consumers from licensed brokers and certified financial planners
who may lack business ethics. These regulatory bodies are the

National Association of Securities Dealers (NASD) and the Securities and Exchange Commission (SEC). The NASD is a self-regulatory body that is extremely strict and thorough. Brokerage firms pay annual fees for membership in the NASD; these dues cover the cost of self-regulation. The SIPC (Securities Investor Protection Corporation) is worth mentioning as well. It is a federal agency that protects investors against failures by brokerage firms (but not against losses from the rise and fall in the market value of investments). Investors' assets are protected up to $500,000, with a limit of $100,000 for cash, so you would get at least that much if your brokerage fails.

The SEC is a federal agency responsible for, among other things, regulating the investment advisory business in the United States. For example, money managers such as mutual fund companies fall under SEC regulation. Most states also have regulatory agencies: In my home state, the Connecticut State Banking Commission is quite impressive.

Checking the references of your broker or financial planner is another method to minimize risks. Talk to clients who have had long relationships with your broker or planner. For every broker who is willing to steal, embezzle, or otherwise take advantage of his or her clients, there are many thousands of financial planners and brokers who provide a great service to their clients. However, negative press sells, so you don't see headlines about people who retire earlier or wealthier than they would have had they not had the help of their financial planner or broker.

MY BROKER SAID THAT HE DID HIS OWN FUNDAMENTAL RESEARCH AND QUANTITATIVE ANALYSIS ON A PARTICULAR INVESTMENT AND, LIKING WHAT HE FOUND, WAS RECOMMENDING IT TO HIS CLIENTS. CAN YOU EXPLAIN WHAT HE WAS TALKING ABOUT?

I can easily understand your confusion. Before I explain what he meant, though, it's important to remember that your broker, planner, insurance agent, and other professional advisors work for you. If you don't understand something they're saying, pin them down. Have them explain it again, and in words you understand.

Many investment companies employ their own research departments that analyze industries and companies. This is fundamental research, often called proprietary research. Much of this research is performed by visiting with and talking to the management of various companies, as well as industry contacts. Performing fundamental research is one way that an investment management group can provide its clients with added value and increase the potential for investment success over time.

Many investment companies also employ their own Quantitative Analysis departments, which are responsible for creating financial models that are used to develop earnings and cash flow projections for particular companies. This information enables the investment firm to evaluate the potential risk/reward associated with investing in a specific company. Therefore, in simple terms, fundamental research can be looked at as the subjective and interpersonal analysis, while quantitative analysis can be thought of as the number-crunching aspect of research.

INDEX